THE FIRESIDE BOOK OF FUN AND GAME SONGS

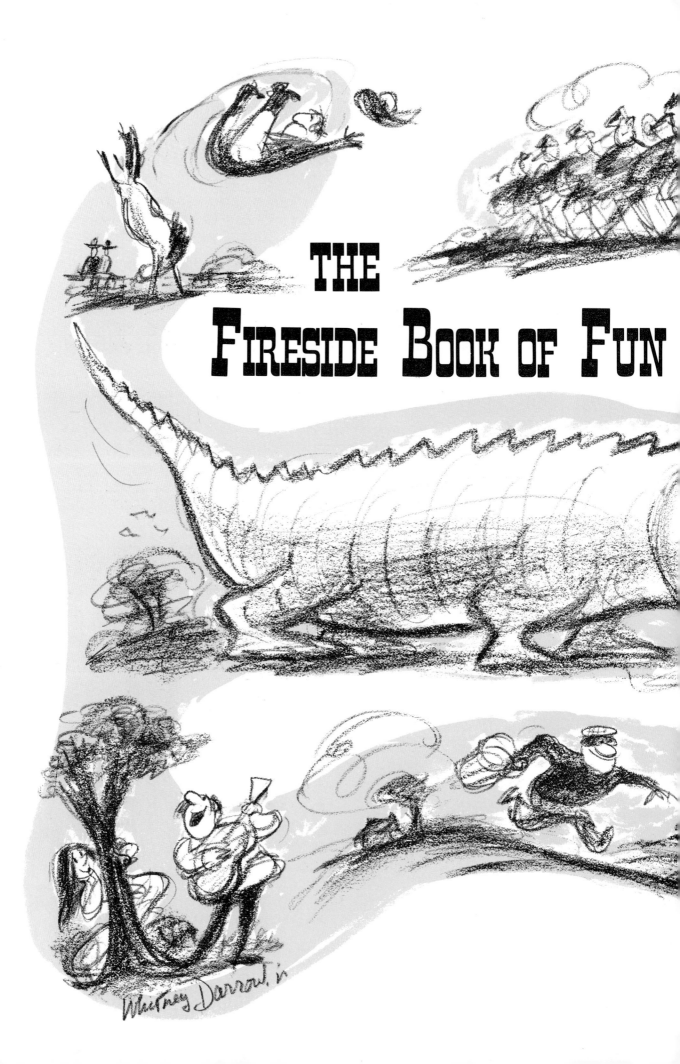

THE FIRESIDE BOOK OF FUN

Whitney Darrow, Jr.

AND GAME SONGS

Collected and Edited by Marie Winn

Musical Arrangements by Allan Miller

Illustrations by Whitney Darrow, Jr.

Simon and Schuster · New York

For help in compiling this book thanks are due to the following:

Mike and Steve Miller, whose indefatigable research at school and camp brought to light some of the best songs in this collection.

Sandy Davis of Camp Killooleet, Vermont, for valuable advice and recommendations.

Janet Malcolm and the Czech School Alumnae Association, for encouragement and expert criticism.

And to Howie Budin, Geraldine Charney, Elinor Jackson, Emilio Cruz—teachers extraordinary at P.S. 84 in New York—and the kids in their classes, who served as splendid guinea pigs for the songs in this collection: this book is gratefully dedicated to you.

PERMISSIONS

Tinga Layo, copyright 1943 by M. Baron Company. Used by permission. *Stately Verse*, from "Favorite Poems Old and New" by Helen Ferris, published by Doubleday & Company, Inc. *The Captain's Shanty* by Elliot Crawford Finch, copyright 1972 by Sarah Lamont and Susan D. Miller. Used by permission. *After the Ball Was Over* and *Springtime in the Rockies* from "The Lore and Language of Schoolchildren" by Iona and Peter Opie, copyright 1959. Used by permission of The Clarendon Press, Oxford. *Rules* and *Me (My Nose Is Blue)*, from "Alexander Soames, His Poems" by Karla Kuskin. Copyright © 1962 by Karla Kuskin. Reprinted by permission of Harper & Row, Publishers, Inc. *The Crocodile* from "Songs and Ballads from Nova Scotia" by Helen Creighton, published by Dover Publications, Inc. *On to the Morgue* from "The American Songbag" by Carl Sandburg, published by Harcourt Brace Jovanovich, Inc. *Nell Flaherty's Drake*, copyright © 1960 by Corinth Books Inc. Reprinted by permission of Corinth Books. *MacTavish* from "Ho! Ho! The Rattlin' Bog" by John Langstaff, published by Harcourt Brace Jovanovich, Inc. *Sweet Potatoes* from "Twice Fifty-five Community Songs." Copyright © 1919, 1929 by Summy-Birchard Company, Evanston, Illinois. Copyright renewed. All rights reserved. Used by permission. *Ducks on a Pond* from "The New Blue Book of Favorite Songs." Used by permission of the publishers, Schmitt, Hall & McCreary Company, Minneapolis, Minn. *The Irish Ballad (Rickety Tickety Tin)* taken from "The Tom Lehrer Song Book" by Tom Lehrer. Copyright © 1954 by Tom Lehrer. Used by permission of Crown Publishers, Inc.

DESIGNED BY JACK JAGET

1   2   3   4   5   6   7   8   9   10

CONTENTS

PART I ONE THING AFTER ANOTHER

Cumulative, diminishing, and catalogue songs

PART II FOLLOW THE LEADER

Echo songs, pattern songs, and songs with easy refrains and choruses

PART III CLAPPING, SNAPPING, AND MAKING PECULIAR NOISES

Motion songs and wordplay songs

PART IV QUESTIONS AND ANSWERS

"He-and-she" songs, and other songs that divide a group into two parts

PART V SPUR OF THE MOMENT

Songs with words, verses, and motions to be improvised on the spot

PART VI HORSING AROUND

Parodies, puns, and sheer nonsense songs

PART VII FUNNY, TALL, AND TRAGICAL TALES

PART VIII GRUESOME, GRISLY, AND MEAN

PART IX FUNNY ROUNDS AND EASY HARMONIES

PART X HELLO, GOODBYE, HURRAY FOR US!

Songs for arriving, cheering, waiting, and leaving

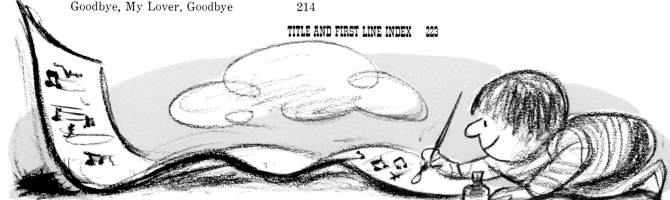

INTRODUCTION

After many years of family and group singing at home and at camps and public schools around the country, we have found that certain songs are surefire hits. These are the songs that invariably "work," to break the ice and win over the hardened, the shy, the bored, or the embarrassed to the joys of singing. Because many of these songs are humorous and many are activity songs that involve some element of play, we have given this category of songs a name: fun and game songs. There are many varieties of fun and game songs, but they all share those qualities of humor and playfulness which make them the most popular songs for group singing.

One kind of fun and game song that may be found among the oldest folk songs is the *cumulative song*, which adds on new words in each successive verse. "The Twelve Days of Christmas" is a familiar example of a *cumulative song*, in which a new gift is added to all the old gifts on each of the twelve days of Christmas. The last verse of a *cumulative song* is always a combination tongue-twister and memory-tester, because the entire accumulation must then be rattled off. Part I of this book includes some familiar and some new *cumulative songs*, as well as a few *catalogue songs*, such as "Mrs. Murphy's Chowder," which have the tongue-twisting and memory-testing characteristics of the *cumulative song* but without the gradual accumulation of words, verse by verse. Thrown in just for fun are a few *diminishing songs*, in which the quantities decrease in each new verse, and one, "Oh the Horse Went Around," in which the song itself actually diminishes during the singing, virtually disappearing into thin air at the end.

While *cumulative* and *catalogue songs* are demanding on the memory, requiring repetitions before they are mastered, the *follow-the-leader songs* in Part II invite singing the first time they are introduced. Among these are songs with simple choruses or refrains that are repeated many times throughout the song. The leader can sing the verses alone when the song is first introduced, but the whole group can join in on the chorus from the start. The easiest *follow-the-leader* songs are *echo songs*, in which each line is echoed exactly throughout the song. "Sippin' Cider Through a Straw" is a favorite example of this type of song. Yet another type of *follow-the-leader* song is the *pattern song*. Here a simple pattern is followed throughout the song with only a small variation of words in each verse. Once the leader has sung one line, the group can join in for the rest of the verse. "Three Jolly Fishermen" is an example of a pattern song, with each verse consisting of a patterned repetition of its first line.

If the success of a song is measured by how often a repetition of it is demanded, then some of the most successful fun and game songs are those that include a physical action. This may involve a single clap at a strategic part of the song, a set of traditional hand motions, or a complete hand-pantomime of the words of the song. Part III contains a variety of *action songs* as well as a few songs in which the fun is focused on an animal sound or a funny noise somewhere in the song.

Dividing a group into parts for back-and-forth singing adds an element of fun and friendly competition to group singing. The *question-and-answer songs* in Part IV all lend themselves to being sung by a group divided into two parts. When the song is a dialogue between a man and a woman, it is logical to divide the group along sex lines. But there is no reason why the boys must always sing the male part and the girls the female part. Indeed, the effect is especially funny when the roles are reversed and the boys sing their part in silly, squeaky voices while the girls try to imitate deep, male voices in their part.

The game aspect of fun and game songs is at its strongest in the *spur-of-the-moment* songs of Part V. All these songs leave room for improvisation of one kind or another. Some require simple rhyming skill, as in "Two Little Blackbirds" or "The Kangaroo." Others require nothing more than a well-developed sense of the ridiculous. A few are constructed around material almost everybody has some knowledge of, such as nursery rhymes or limericks, allowing each person in the group to contribute verses of his own choosing. These are songs that can go on and on, if the group is in the right mood, until the voices give out.

The *parody* and *nonsense songs* in Part VI belong to an old tradition of folk humor usually passed along from generation to generation by schoolchildren. Grown-ups often feel obliged to groan at these songs, but their furtive delight in them is hard to hide. Some of these songs, such as "After the Ball Was Over," parody specific popular songs of the past, while others laugh at a whole genre of song, as does "The Captain's Shanty" or "The Song of the Salvation Army."

Part VII contains songs that tell funny stories or tall tales. Some of these are complicated *virtuoso songs,* the songs that people demand the words for, in order to become the stars of future singing sessions. "Bluebeard" and "Bible Stories" are examples of *virtuoso songs.* Other story songs are simpler to learn and may be easily picked up by a group after one or two repetitions. It is the humor of the story itself that forms the attraction of these songs, especially if it is mildly tinged with tragedy, as in "The Ship *Titanic*" or "Dunderbeck."

Then there are the songs that are blatantly gruesome and bloodthirsty. That these are often the alltime favorites of any group need not be construed as a reflection of the basic nastiness of human nature, but only of the human need to laugh at what is frightening. Part VIII presents a number of cheerful songs describing a variety of antisocial behavior ranging from simple meanness to murder and cannibalism, as well as a number of songs lightly commenting on man's mortality.

Singing in harmony adds a new dimension of enjoyment to group singing. The fun, in this case, does not depend on the words of a song; it lies in the music itself. One of the easiest and most popular ways of creating harmonies in a group is by means of *rounds.* Everybody learns one simple melody. Then, when the group is divided into parts and each starts a measure or two after the last, pleasing harmonies seem to "happen," without any harmonizing skill on the part of the singers. While all rounds are fun to sing, Part IX includes only songs that have some element of fun in the words as well, to compound the enjoyment they offer a group. This section also includes several songs such as "Sweet Potatoes" with a descant line simple enough to be learned quickly by an inexperienced group.

The joys of arriving at a destination are heightened and the sorrows of parting are relieved by group singing. Part X includes *occasional songs*—for arriving, for departing, for waiting at mealtimes and other occasions. It also offers a few songs that declare, "Hurray for us!" in one way or another, for a group to sing to a rival group, or simply for its members to let one another know that they feel great, that they feel great because they are all together, and that singing together is great fun.

There is a vast literature of songs to be sung that may be more profound or beautiful or more musically interesting than many of the songs in this book. But before these beauties and profundities can be experienced, there has to be the willingness to sing, the feeling that singing is delightful and gratifying. Fun and game songs bring about this feeling as no other songs can do. Therein lies their greatest value.

But fun and game songs need no defense. Their popularity will always counterbalance any shortcomings. These are the songs people choose to sing at picnics and clambakes and cook-outs. They are the songs kids traditionally sing at summer camps, and bring home to their friends and family. We have had a great deal of fun singing these songs together. We would like to share them here with you.

PART I
ONE THING AFTER ANOTHER

Cumulative, diminishing, and catalogue songs

The Court of King Carraticus

An amusing cumulative song of obscure origin. In each verse a new description is added to the court of King Carraticus. The last verse adds a surprise twist.

Rhythmic and bouncy

1. Oh, the court of King Car - ra - ti - cus is just pas - sing by; Oh, the
2. Oh, the { ha - rem of the
court of King Car -

court of King Car - ra - ti - cus is just pas - sing by; Oh, the
{ ha - rem of the
court of King Car -

court of King Car - ra - ti - cus is just pas - sing by; Oh, the
{ ha - rem of the
court of King Car -

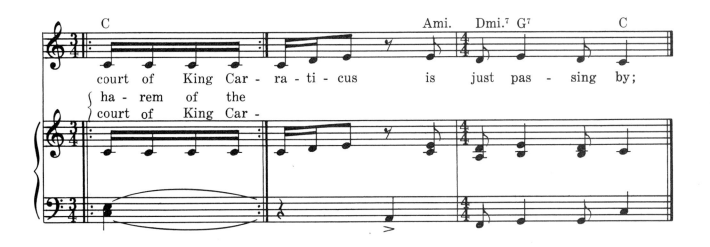

court of King Car - ra - ti - cus   is just pas - sing by;
ha - rem of the
court of King Car -

3. Oh; the ladies of the harem of the court of King Carraticus
   are just passing by;
  Oh, the ladies of the harem of the court of King Carraticus
   are just passing by;
  Oh, the ladies of the harem of the court of King Carraticus
   are just passing by;
  Oh, the ladies of the harem of the court of King Carraticus
   are just passing by.

4. Oh, the faces of the ladies of the harem of the court of
  King Carraticus are just passing by
  (repeat three more times).

5. Oh, the noses of the faces of the ladies of the harem of
  the court of King Carraticus are just passing by
  (repeat three more times).

6. Oh, the boys who put the powder on the noses of the faces of
  the ladies of the harem of the court of King Carraticus
  are just passing by
  (repeat three more times).

7. Oh, the scintillating stitches on the britches of the boys who
  put the powder on the noses of the faces of the ladies
  of the harem of the court of King Carraticus
  are just passing by
  (repeat three more times).

8. Oh, the fascinating witches put the scintillating stitches
  on the britches of the boys who put the powder
  on the noses of the faces of the ladies of the
  harem of the court of King Carraticus are just
  passing by
  (repeat three more times).

9. If you want to take a photo of the fascinating witches put
  the scintillating stitches on the britches of the
  boys who put the powder on the noses of the faces
  of the ladies of the harem of the court of King
  Carraticus . . .
  Spoken: It's too late! They just passed by!

Wiggle the Wool

Point to the appropriate part of the body as you sing this song—in order, from the beginning: the head, the eyelids, nose, mouth, teeth, stomach. A sweeping gesture indicating everything else is used for the last verse. Shake head wildly at the words "wiggle the wool" in all verses.

With my hands and my fin - gers, oh, what have I here?

1. This is my top - not - cher, noth - ing to fear. 1. Top - not - cher.
2. These are my eye - blin - kers, 2. Eye blin - kers, top - not - cher.

Wig - gle   the   wool!   That's what   they   taught me   in   school.

last time

3. With my hands and my fingers, oh, what have I here?
   This is my sneeze-maker, nothing to fear.
   Sneeze-maker, eye-blinkers, topnotcher. Wiggle the wool!
   That's what they taught me in school.

4. With my hands and my fingers, oh, what have I here?
   This is my soup-strainer, nothing to fear.
   Soup-strainer, sneeze-maker, eye-blinkers, topnotcher.
      Wiggle the wool!
   That's what they taught me in school.

5. With my hands and my fingers, oh, what have I here?
   These are my glop-choppers, nothing to fear.
   Glop-choppers, soup-strainer, sneeze-maker, eye-blinkers,
      topnotcher. Wiggle the wool!
   That's what they taught me in school.

6. With my hands and my fingers, oh, what have I here?
   This is my breadbasket, nothing to fear.
   Breadbasket, glop-choppers, soup-strainer, sneeze-maker,
      eye-blinkers, topnotcher. Wiggle the wool!
   That's what they taught me in school.

7. With my hands and my fingers, oh, what have I here?
   This is my et cetera, nothing to fear.
   Et cetera, breadbasket, glop-choppers, soup-strainer,
      sneeze-maker, eye-blinkers, topnotcher. Wiggle the wool!
   That's what they taught me in school.

There's a Hole in the Middle of the Sea

*Some cumulative songs repeat the accumulation once in each verse.
In this song it is repeated three times!*

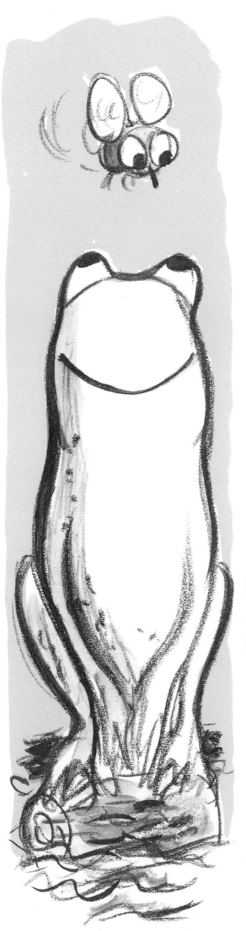

Relentlessly

1. There's a hole in the mid-dle of the sea.
2. There's a { log in the / hole in the } mid-dle of the sea.

There's a hole in the mid-dle of the sea.
There's a { log in the / hole in the } mid-dle of the sea.

There's a hole, _____ there's a hole,
There's a log, _____ there's a log,

There's a hole in the mid-dle of the sea.

There's a ⎰log in the⎱ mid-dle of the sea.
         ⎱hole in the⎰

3. There's a bump on the log in the hole in the middle of the sea.
   There's a bump on the log in the hole in the middle of the sea.
   There's a bump, there's a bump,
   There's a bump on the log in the hole in the middle of the sea.

4. There's a frog on the bump on the log in the hole in the
      middle of the sea.
   There's a frog on the bump on the log in the hole in the
      middle of the sea.
   There's a frog, there's a frog,
   There's a frog on the bump on the log in the hole in the
      middle of the sea.

5. There's a fly on the frog on the bump on the log in the hole
      in the middle of the sea.
   There's a fly on the frog on the bump on the log in the hole
      in the middle of the sea.
   There's a fly, there's a fly,
   There's a fly on the frog on the bump on the log in the hole
      in the middle of the sea.

6. There's a wing on the fly on the frog on the bump on the log
      in the hole in the middle of the sea.
   There's a wing on the fly on the frog on the bump on the log
      in the hole in the middle of the sea.
   There's a wing, there's a wing,
   There's a wing on the fly on the frog on the bump on the log
      in the hole in the middle of the sea.

7. There's a flea on the wing on the fly on the frog on the bump
      on the log in the hole in the middle of the sea.
   There's a flea on the wing on the fly on the frog on the bump
      on the log in the hole in the middle of the sea.
   There's a flea, there's a flea,
   There's a flea on the wing on the fly on the frog on the bump
      on the log in the hole in the middle of the sea.

Mrs. Murphy's Chowder

A good catalogue song to sing on an empty stomach.

Rowdy

Won't you bring back, won't you bring back Mis - sus Mur-phy's chow-der? It was
tune - ful. Ev- 'ry spoon-ful made you yo - del loud - er.
Af - ter din - ner, Un - cle Ben used to fill his foun - tain pen

From a plate of Mis-sus Mur phy's chow - der.

Chorus
Faster

It had ice cream, cold cream, ben-zine, gas-o-line, Soup beans, string beans, float-ing all a-round;
Sponge cake, beef-steak, mis-take, stom-ach ache, Cream puffs, ear-muffs, man-y to be found;

Silk hats, door-mats, bed slats, Dem-o-crats; Cow-bells, door-bells beck-on you to dine;

Meat-balls, fish balls, moth-balls, can-non-balls. Come on in; the chow-der's fine!

2. Won't you bring back, won't you bring back Missus Murphy's
chowder?
From each helping you'll be yelping for a headache powder,
And if they had it where you are, you might find a trolley car
In a plate of Missus Murphy's chowder.

3. Won't you bring back, won't you bring back Missus Murphy's
chowder?
You can pack it, you can stack it all around the larder.
The plumber died the other day; they embalmed him right away
In a bowl of Missus Murphy's chowder.

Chorus

Chorus: It had ice cream, cold cream, benzine,
gasoline,
Soup beans, string beans floating all
around;
Sponge cake, beefsteak, mistake,
stomach ache,
Cream puffs, earmuffs, many to be
found;
Silk hats, doormats, bed slats,
Democrats;
Cowbells, doorbells beckon you to dine;
Meatballs, fish balls, mothballs, cannon
balls.
Come on in; the chowder's fine.

The Green Grass Grows All Around

This song is often sung as a game: members of the group take turns singing the last line of the verses, which begins with "Oh..." Whoever makes a mistake in the order of accumulation is out.

With invention (Vary the left hand from verse to verse, and within the verses. Some variations have been indicated. Make up more of your own.)

1. There was a tree (There was a tree) All in the wood (All in the wood),
2. Now, on that tree (Now on that tree) There was a trunk (There was a trunk,

The pret - tiest lit - tle tree (The pret - tiest lit - tle tree)
The pret - tiest lit - tle trunk (The pret - tiest lit - tle trunk)

That you ev - er did see (That you ev - er did see).
That you ev - er did see (That you ev - er did see).

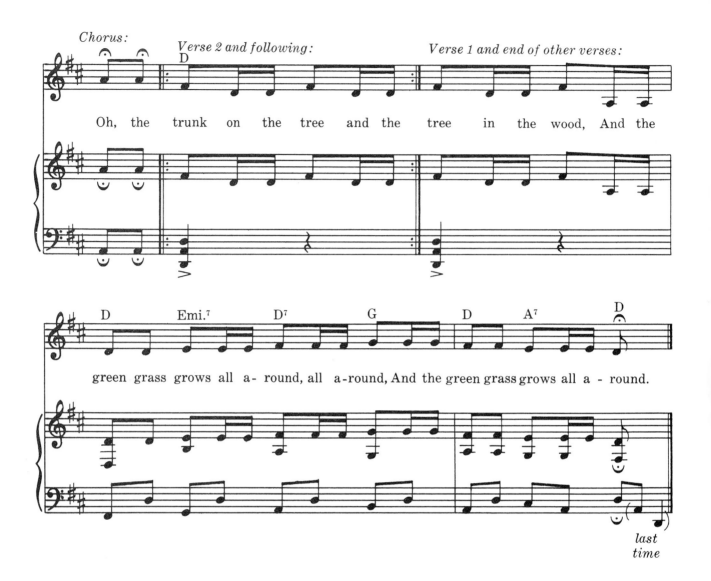

Chorus: *Verse 2 and following:*   *Verse 1 and end of other verses:*

Oh, the trunk on the tree and the tree in the wood, And the green grass grows all a- round, all a-round, And the green grass grows all a - round.

last time

3.
Now, on that trunk (Now on that trunk)
There was a limb (There was a limb),
The prettiest little limb (The prettiest little limb)
That you ever did see (That you ever did see).
Oh, the limb on the trunk
  and the trunk on the tree
  and the tree in the wood

Chorus And the green grass grows all around,
   all around,
  And the green grass grows all around.

5.
Now, on that branch (Now, on that branch)
There was a nest (There was a nest),
The prettiest little nest (The prettiest little nest)
That you ever did see (That you ever did see).
Oh, the nest on the branch
  and the branch on the limb
  and the limb on the trunk
  and the trunk on the tree
  and the tree in the wood   *Chorus*

4.
Now, on that limb (Now, on that limb)
There was a branch (There was a branch),
The prettiest little branch
  (The prettiest little branch)
That you ever did see (That you ever did see).
Oh, the branch on the limb
  and the limb on the trunk
  and the trunk on the tree
  and the tree in the wood   *Chorus*

6.
And in the nest (And in the nest)
There was an egg (There was an egg),
The prettiest little egg (The prettiest little egg)
That you ever did see (That you ever did see).
Oh, the egg in the nest
  and the nest on the branch
  and the branch on the limb
  and the limb on the trunk
  and the trunk on the tree
  and the tree in the wood   *Chorus*

7.

And in the egg (And in the egg)
There was a bird (There was a bird),
The prettiest little bird (The prettiest little bird)
That you ever did see (That you ever did see).
Oh, the bird in the egg
   and the egg in the nest
   and the nest on the branch
   and the branch on the limb
   and the trunk on the tree
   and the tree in the wood   *Chorus*

8.

And on the bird (And on the bird)
There was a feather (There was a feather),
The prettiest little feather (The prettiest little feather)
That you ever did see (That you ever did see).
Oh, the feather on the bird
   and the bird in the egg
   and the egg in the nest
   and the nest on the branch
   and the branch on the limb
   and the limb on the trunk
   and the trunk on the tree
   and the tree in the wood   *Chorus*

9.

And from the feather (And from the feather)
There was a bed (There was a bed),
The prettiest little bed (The prettiest little bed)
That you ever did see (That you ever did see).
Oh, the bed from the feather
   and the feather on the bird
   and the bird in the egg
   and the egg in the nest
   and the nest on the branch
   and the branch on the limb
   and the limb on the trunk
   and the trunk on the tree
   and the tree in the wood   *Chorus*

10.

And on the bed (And on the bed)
There was a child (There was a child),
The prettiest little child (The prettiest little child)
That you ever did see (That you ever did see).
Oh, the child on the bed
   and the bed from the feather
   and the feather on the bird
   and the bird in the egg
   and the egg in the nest
   and the nest on the branch
   and the branch on the limb
   and the limb on the trunk
   and the trunk on the tree
   and the tree in the wood   *Chorus*

11.

And then the child (And then the child)
He planted a seed (He planted a seed),
The prettiest little seed (The prettiest little seed)
That you ever did see (That you ever did see).
Oh, the seed from the child.
   and the child on the bed
   and the bed from the feather
   and the feather on the bird
   and the bird in the egg
   and the egg in the nest
   and the nest on the branch
   and the branch on the limb
   and the limb on the trunk
   and the trunk on the tree
   and the tree in the wood   *Chorus*

12.

And from that seed (And from that seed)
There grew a tree (There grew a tree),
The prettiest little tree (The prettiest little tree)
That you ever did see (That you ever did see).
Oh, the tree from the seed
   and the seed from the child
   and the child on the bed
   and the bed from the feather
   and the feather on the bird
   and the bird in the egg
   and the egg in the nest
   and the nest on the branch
   and the branch on the limb
   and the limb on the trunk
   and the trunk on the tree
   and the tree in the wood   *Chorus*

Once an Austrian Went Yodeling

In each verse of this song a new sound and motion are added to the chorus to represent the new person, animal, or natural disaster met by the yodeling Austrian. The last verse ends the song with a surprise.

With great rhythmic emphasis

1. Once an Aus - tri - an went yo - del-ing on a moun - tain so high, When he
2. Once an Aus - tri - an went yo - del-ing on a moun - tain so high, When he

met with an av - a - lanche, In - ter - rup - ting his cry.
met with a ski - er, In - ter - rup - ting his cry.

Chorus (for motions, see below):

Oh, la - dee Yo - del - lay - hit - tee, A - yo - del - lay- cuc - koo, cuc - koo,

Spoken:

1. Rum - ble   rum - ble,
2. { Rum - ble   rum - ble,   Yo - del - lay - hit - tee - a - lo.
   { Whoosh!

F

3. Once an Austrian went yodeling
   On a mountain so high,
   When he met with a St. Bernard
   Interrupting his cry.

   Chorus: Oh, lay-dee *(rapid hand-patting of*
                 knees, like galloping)
              Yodel-lay-hittee,
                 (pat—clap—finger-snap)
              A-yodel-lay-cuckoo, cuckoo,
                 (pat—clap—snap—snap)
              Rumble rumble *(hands rotate like*
                 wheels turning, for avalanche),
              Whoosh! *(hand makes swooping,*
                 roller-coaster movement for skier)
              Arf arf *(hands up in begging position*
                 for St. Bernard),
              Yodel-lay-hittee-a-lo.

4. Once an Austrian went yodeling
   On a mountain so high,
   When he met with a grizzly bear,
   Interrupting his cry.
   (Continue hand motions in each verse)

   Chorus: Oh, lay-dee
              Yodel-lay-hittee,
              A-yodel-lay-cuckoo, cuckoo,
              Rumble rumble,
              Whoosh!
              Arf arf,
              Rargh! *(hands up with fingers like*
                 claws in a menacing position, for
                 grizzly bear)
              Yodel-lay-hittee-a-lo.

5. Once an Austrian went yodeling
   On a mountain so high,
   When he met with a milking maid,
   Interrupting his cry.

   Chorus: Oh, lay-dee
              Yodel-lay-hittee,
              A-yodel-lay-cuckoo, cuckoo,
              Rumble rumble,
              Whoosh!
              Arf arf,
              Rargh!
              Psst psst *(hands alternate in milking*
                 motion),
              Yodel-lay-hittee-a-lo.

6. Once an Austrian went yodeling
   On a mountain so high,
   When he met with a dinosaur,
   Interrupting his cry.

   Chorus: Oh, lay-dee
              Yodel-lay-hittee,
              A-yodel-lay-cuckoo, cuckoo,
              Rumble rumble,
              Whoosh!
              Arf, arf,
              Rargh!
              Psst psst,
              Eeeeeeeeeeeee! *(everyone shrieks*
                 wildly and falls on the ground in a
                 heap).

She'll Be Coming Round the Mountain

A railroading song from the 1870's that has become one of our most famil-
iar folk songs. Each verse contains an exclamation (Toot toot! etc.), and at
the end of each line the exclamations of all preceding verses are sung in
backward order.

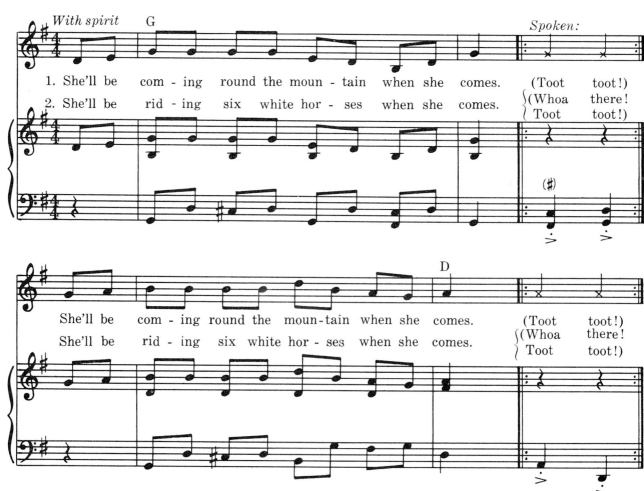

With spirit G

1. She'll be com - ing round the moun - tain when she comes. (Toot toot!)
2. She'll be rid - ing six white hor - ses when she comes. (Whoa there! Toot toot!)

D

She'll be com - ing round the moun-tain when she comes. (Toot toot!)
She'll be rid - ing six white hor - ses when she comes. (Whoa there! Toot toot!)

Spoken:

She'll be com-ing round the moun-tain, she'll be com-ing round the moun-tain, She'll be
She'll be rid-ing six white hor-ses, she'll be rid-ing six white hor-ses, She'll be

com-ing round the moun-tain when she comes. (Toot toot!)
rid-ing six white hor-ses when she comes. {(Whoa there!
Toot toot!)

3. And we'll all come out to see her when she comes. (Hi, babe!
   Whoa there! Toot toot!)
   And we'll all come out to see her when she comes. (Hi, babe!
   Whoa there! Toot toot!)
   And we'll all come out to see her, and we'll all come out
   to see her,
   And we'll all come out to see her when she comes. (Hi, babe!
   Whoa there! Toot toot!)

4. And we'll all have chicken and dumplings when she comes.
   (Yum yum! Hi, babe! Whoa there! Toot toot!)
   And we'll all have chicken and dumplings when she comes.
   (Yum yum! Hi, babe! Whoa there! Toot toot!)
   And we'll all have chicken and dumplings, and we'll all
   have chicken and dumplings,
   And we'll all have chicken and dumplings when she comes.
   (Yum yum! Hi, babe! Whoa there! Toot toot!)

5. And we'll wear our red pajamas when she comes. (Scratch scratch!
   Yum yum! Hi, babe! Whoa there! Toot toot!)
   And we'll wear our red pajamas when she comes. (Scratch scratch!
   Yum yum! Hi, babe! Whoa there! Toot toot!)
   And we'll wear our red pajamas, and we'll wear our red pajamas,
   And we'll wear our red pajamas when she comes. (Scratch scratch!
   Yum yum! Hi, babe! Whoa there! Toot toot!)

The Twelve Days of Christmas

A very old cumulative carol from England. The twelve days of Christmas are those between Christmas Day and Epiphany.

tree.   3. On the third day of Christ-mas, my true love gave to me   Three French hens,

two tur - tle - doves, and a par - tridge ___ in a pear tree.   4. On the

fourth day of Christ - mas my true love gave to me   {Four call - ing birds,
{Three French ___ hens,

two tur - tle - doves, And a par - tridge in a pear tree.   5. On the

fifth day of Christ-mas, my true love gave to me Five gold _____ rings,

four cal-ling birds, three French hens, two _____ tur-tle-doves, And a

par-tridge _____ in a pear tree.
6. On the sixth day of Christ-mas, my
7. On the seventh
8. On the etc.

true love gave to me
6. Six geese a-lay-ing, five gold _____
7. Seven swans a-swim-ming
8. etc.

rings, four — cal - ling birds, three French hens,

two — tur - tle - doves, And a par - tridge — in a pear tree.

Dal segno

8. On the eighth day of Christmas, my true love sent to me,
   eight maids a-milking,

9. On the ninth day of Christmas, my true love sent to me,
   nine ladies dancing,

10. On the tenth day of Christmas, my true love sent to me,
    ten lords a-leaping, etc.

11. On the eleventh day of Christmas, my true love sent to me,
    eleven pipers piping, etc.

12. On the twelfth day of Christmas, my true love sent to me,
    twelve drummers drumming,
    eleven pipers piping,
    ten lords a-leaping,
    nine ladies dancing,
    eight maids a-milking,
    seven swans a-swimming,
    six geese a-laying,
    five gold rings, four calling birds, three French hens,
    two turtle doves, and a partridge in a pear tree.

29

Oh, the Horse Went Around

This song is most effective with a group if there are no advance explanations, letting people catch on to the joke gradually.

Start moderately, get faster and faster

1. Oh, the horse went a - round with his foot off the ground. Oh, the horse went a - round with his foot off the ground. Oh, the horse went a - round with his foot off the ground. Oh, the

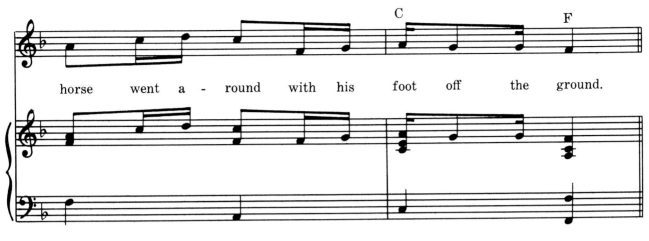

horse went a - round with his foot off the ground.

Chorus (spoken):

Next time, we sing this verse Just a lit - tle bit fast-er and a lit - tle bit worse.

2. Oh, the horse went around with his foot off the
Oh, the horse went around with his foot off the
Oh, the horse went around with his foot off the
Oh, the horse went around with his foot off the

   Chorus (spoken): Next time, we sing this verse
   Just a little bit faster and a little bit worse.

3. Oh, the horse went around with his foot off
Oh, the horse went around with his foot off
Oh, the horse went around with his foot off
Oh, the horse went around with his foot off

   Chorus

4. Oh, the horse went around with his foot
Oh, the horse went around with his foot
Oh, the horse went around with his foot
Oh, the horse went around with his foot

   Chorus

5. Oh, the horse went around with his
Oh, the horse went around with his
Oh, the horse went around with his
Oh, the horse went around with his

   Chorus

6. Oh, the horse went around with
Oh, the horse went around with
Oh, the horse went around with
Oh, the horse went around with

   Chorus

7. Oh, the horse went around
Oh, the horse went around
Oh, the horse went around
Oh, the horse went around

   Chorus

8. Oh, the horse went
Oh, the horse went
Oh, the horse went
Oh, the horse went

   Chorus

9. Oh, the horse
Oh, the horse
Oh, the horse
Oh, the horse

   Chorus

10. Oh, the   11. Oh,
    Oh, the   Oh,
    Oh, the   Oh,
    Oh, the   Oh,

    Chorus   *Chorus*

12. Complete silence while everybody thinks
    the song through to himself.
    End song with a final rendition
    of verse 1.

Green Bottles

Start at any number of bottles and continue singing until there are none left. The fun of this song depends on the sound effects that follow the third line.

With annoying gusto

There are ten green bot-tles a-stand-ing on the wall;

There are ten green bot-tles a-stand-ing on the wall.

But if one green bot-tle should ac-ci-dent-'ly fall, *Spoken:* Crash!

There'd be nine green bot-tles a-stand-ing on the wall;

2. There are nine green bottles astanding on the wall;
   There are nine green bottles astanding on the wall.
   But if one green bottle should accident'ly fall [Spoken], Crash!
   There'd be eight green bottles astanding on the wall.

   (Continue until there are no green bottles astanding
      on the wall.)

*Pianist slurs D to B♭, then two-fisted cluster for crash—different for each verse.
†After last verse pianist makes crash on keys with both forearms.

Roll Over, Roll Over

A good joke that misfires.

Rollicking

1. {Nine men slept in a board-ing-house bed, Roll o - ver, roll o - ver. They
all rolled o - ver when an - y - one said, "Roll o - ver, roll o - ver."

One of them thought it would be a good joke Not to roll o - ver when

an - y - one spoke, And in the scuf-fle his neck got broke, Roll o - ver, roll o - ver.

2. Eight men slept in a boardinghouse bed,
Roll over, roll over.
They all rolled over when anyone said,
"Roll over, roll over."
One of them thought it would be a good joke
Not to roll over when anyone spoke,
And in the scuffle his neck got broke,
Roll over, roll over.

3. Seven men slept in a boardinghouse bed,
Roll over, roll over.
They all rolled over when anyone said,
"Roll over, roll over."
One of them thought it would be a good joke
Not to roll over when anyone spoke,
And in the scuffle his neck got broke,
Roll over, roll over.

4–9. Continue until song concludes abruptly with words "One man slept in
a boardinghouse bed."

Hush, Little Baby

A favorite catalogue song that has been challenging memories for generations.

1. Hush, lit-tle ba-by, don't say a word. Ma-ma's gon-na buy you a mock-ing-bird. And if that mock-ing-bird don't sing, Ma-ma's gon-na buy you a dia-mond ring.

2. And If that dia-mond ring turn brass, Ma-ma's gon-na buy you a look-ing glass. And if that look-ing glass get broke, Ma-ma's gon-na buy you a bil-ly goat.

3. And if that billy goat don't pull,
   Mama's gonna buy you a cart and bull.
   And if that cart and bull turn over,
   Mama's gonna buy you a dog named Rover.

4. And if that dog named Rover don't bark,
   Mama's gonna buy you a horse and cart.
   And if that horse and cart fall down,
   You'll still be the sweetest little baby in town.

PART II
FOLLOW THE LEADER

Echo songs, pattern songs,
and songs with easy refrains and choruses

Sippin' Cider Through a Straw

A cagey suitor gets his comeuppance in the last verse
of this old favorite echo song.

I. The pret - ti - est girl II. (The pret - ti - est girl) I ev - er

saw (I ev - er saw) was sip - pin' ci - (Was sip - pin' ci -) Der through a

straw. (Der through a straw.) The pret - ti - est girl I ev - er

saw _____ was sip - pin' ci - der through a straw. _____

2. I asked that girl (I asked that girl),
"How do you draw ("How do you draw)
That apple ci- (That apple ci-)
Der through a straw?" (Der through a straw?")
I asked that girl, "How do you draw
That apple cider through a straw?"

3. She smiled at me (She smiled at me)
And said that I (And said that I)
Might come up close (Might come up close)
And give a try. (And give a try.)
She smiled at me and said that I
Might come up close and give a try.

4. And cheek to cheek (And cheek to cheek)
And jaw to jaw (And jaw to jaw),
We sipped that ci- (We sipped that ci-)
Der through a straw. (Der through a straw.)
And cheek to cheek and jaw to jaw,
We sipped that cider through a straw.

5. And all at once (And all at once)
That straw did slip. (That straw did slip.)
I sipped some ci- (I sipped some ci-)
Der from her lip. (Der from her lip.)
And all at once that straw did slip.
I sipped some cider from her lip.

6. And now I've got (And now I've got)
A mother-in-law (A mother-in-law)
From sippin' ci- (From sippin' ci-)
Der through a straw. (Der through a straw.)
And now I've got a mother-in-law
From sippin' cider through a straw.

These Bones Gonna Rise Again

A very colloquial version of the Adam-and-Eve story, with a refrain after every verse line and a rousing chorus between verses.

1. The { Lord he thought he'd make a man; / Made him out-a dirt and a lit-tle bit o' sand. } These bones gon-na rise a-gain.

Chorus:
I know'd it, know'd it, In-deed I know'd it know'd it, I know'd it, know'd it: These bones___ gon-na rise a-gain.

2. Adam was the first he made;
Refrain:
These bones gonna rise again.
Put him on the bank and laid him in the shade.
Refrain:
These bones gonna rise again.

   Chorus: I know'd it, know'd it,
   Indeed I know'd it, know'd it,
   I know'd it, know'd it:
   These bones gonna rise again.

3. Thought he'd make a woman too; (*Refrain*)
Didn't know 'xactly what to do. (*Refrain*)
Chorus

4. Took a rib from Adam's side; (*Refrain*)
Made Miss Eve for to be his bride. (*Refrain*)
Chorus

5. Put 'em in a garden rich and fair; (*Refrain*)
Told them they might eat whatever was there.
(*Refrain*)
Chorus

6. But to one tree they must not go; (*Refrain*)
Must leave the apples there to grow. (*Refrain*)
Chorus

7. Old Miss Eve come walkin' 'round; (*Refrain*)
Spied a tree all loaded down. (*Refrain*)
Chorus

8. Serpent coiled around a chunk; (*Refrain*)
At Miss Eve his eye he wunk. (*Refrain*)
Chorus

9. First she took a little pull; (*Refrain*)
Then she filled her apron full. (*Refrain*)
Chorus

10. Adam took a little slice; (*Refrain*)
Smacked his lips and said, "Real nice!" (*Refrain*)
Chorus

11. The Lord he come awand'rin' 'round; (*Refrain*)
Spied them peelings on the ground. (*Refrain*)
Chorus

12. The Lord he rose up in his wrath; (*Refrain*)
Told 'em, "Beat it down the path!" (*Refrain*)
Chorus

13. "Out of this garden you must git; (*Refrain*)
Earn your living by your sweat." (*Refrain*)
Chorus

14. He put an angel by the door; (*Refrain*)
Told 'em not to come back anymore. (*Refrain*)
Chorus:

15. Of this tale there ain't no more; (*Refrain*)
Eve ate the apple, gave Adam the core. (*Refrain*)

   Chorus: I know'd it, know'd it,
   Indeed I know'd it, know'd it,
   I know'd it—wheeee!
   These bones gonna rise again.

One More River

*There are many versions of this song, but
only one with the following irreverent ending.*

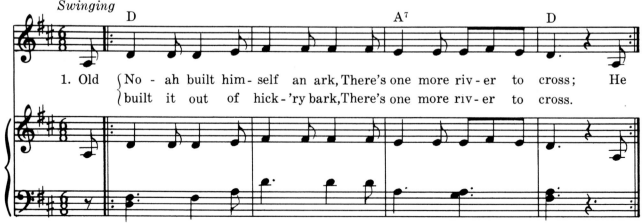

1. Old {No - ah built him - self an ark, There's one more riv - er to cross; He
built it out of hick - 'ry bark, There's one more riv - er to cross.

Chorus

One more riv - er, _____ And that's the riv - er of Jor - dan;

One more riv - er, _____ There's one more riv - er to cross.

2. The animals went in one by one,
   There's one more river to cross.
   The elephant chewed on a hot cross bun,
   There's one more river to cross.

   Chorus:　One more river,
   　　　　　And that's the river of Jordan;
   　　　　　One more river,
   　　　　　There's one more river to cross.

3. The animals went in two by two,
   There's one more river to cross;
   The anteater and the kangaroo,
   There's one more river to cross.
   Chorus

4. The animals went in three by three,
   There's one more river to cross;
   The monkey and the chimpanzee,
   There's one more river to cross.
   Chorus

5. The animals went in four by four,
   There's one more river to cross;
   The hippopotamus stuck in the door,
   There's one more river to cross.
   Chorus

6. The animals went in five by five,
   There's one more river to cross;
   Noah's sons and all their wives,
   There's one more river to cross.
   Chorus

7. And as they talked of this and that,
   There's one more river to cross;
   The ark bumped into Mount Ararat,
   There's one more river to cross.
   Chorus

8. Oh, Mrs. Noah she got drunk,
   There's one more river to cross;
   And kicked the old gentleman out of his bunk,
   There's one more river to cross.
   Chorus

The E-ri-e Canal

It's pronounced Ee-rye-ee in this old canal song, perhaps in reference to rye whiskey.

With rhythmic emphasis

1. We were for-ty miles from Al-ba-ny, For - get it I nev-er
2. We were loa-ded down with bar - ley, We were loa-ded down with

shall: What a ter-ri-ble storm we had one night On the E - ri - e Ca-nal.
rye; And the cap - tain he looked down at me with his bea-dy lit-tle eye.

Chorus:

Oh, the E - ri - e is a-ri - sing, And the gin's a-get-ting

low, And I scarce - ly think we'll get a ____ drink Till we

get to Buf - fa - lo, _____ Till we get to Buf - fa - lo.

3. Well the captain he comes up on deck
   With a spyglass in his hand,
   But the fog it was so awful thick
   That he couldn't spy the land.

   Chorus: Oh, the E-ri-e is a-rising,
   And the gin's a-getting low,
   And I scarcely think we'll get a drink
   Till we get to Buffalo.
   Till we get to Buffalo.

4. Well the cook she was a grand old gal,
   And she had a ragged dress,
   So we hoisted her upon a pole
   As a signal of distress.

   Chorus

5. Well, the captain he got married,
   And the cook she went to jail,
   And I'm the only son-of-a-gun
   That's left to tell the tale.

   Chorus

Gideon's Band

*A minstrel song from the 1870's that seems to start out as a joke, grows
serious in the middle, and reveals its true nature in the last verse.*

Bright and bouncy

1. Oh, keep your hat up-on your head, Oh, keep your hat up-on your head, Oh,
2. Oh, keep your nose up-on your face, Oh, keep your nose up-on your face, Oh,

keep your hat up-on your head, Oh, keep your hat up-on your head.
keep your nose up-on your face, Oh, keep your nose up-on your face.

Chorus:

If you be-long to Gid-e-on's Band, Oh, here's my heart and here's my hand. If

you be-long to Gid-e-on's Band, We're hunt-ing for a home.____

3. Oh, keep your coat upon your back,
   Oh, keep your coat upon your back,
   Oh, keep your coat upon your back :
   You'll need it on that upward track.

Chorus: If you belong to Gideon's band,
   Oh, here's my heart and here's my hand.
   If you belong to Gideon's band,
   We're hunting for a home.

4. Oh, keep your pants upon your legs,
   Oh, keep your pants upon your legs,
   Oh, keep your pants upon your legs,
   To hang them on those golden pegs.

   Chorus

5. Oh, keep your shoes upon your feet,
   Oh, keep your shoes upon your feet,
   Oh, keep your shoes upon your feet,
   To walk upon that golden street.

   Chorus

6. Oh, keep your toenails on the ground,
   Oh, keep your toenails on the ground,
   Oh, keep your toenails on the ground,
   That when you're wanted, you'll be found.

   Chorus

7. Twixt you and I, I really think,
   Twixt you and I, I really think,
   Twixt you and I, I really think,
   It's pretty near time to take a drink.

   Chorus

Haul Away, Joe

An example of the short-drag sea shanty, sung on occasions when only short, strong pulls were required. At the last syllable of each chorus, all hands would give one great, mighty pull, whereupon the shantyman would immediately start the next verse. The song is most effective in group singing when different singers take turns with the verses, while the whole group joins in loudly with the chorus.

1. When I was a lit - tle lad, and so my mo - ther told me,
2. King Lou - is was the king of France be - fore the re - vo - lu - tion.

Chorus:

Way, haul a - way, we'll haul a - way, Joe!

Emi.   Dmi.   Ami.

1. That if I did not kiss the girls, my lips would grow all mol - dy. ___
2. But then he got his head chopped off, which spoiled his con - sti - tu - tion. ___

Emi.   Dmi. Emi. Ami.

Way, haul a - way, we'll haul a - way, Joe!

3. Oh, once I had a Boston girl, and she was fat and lazy.
   Chorus: Way, haul away, we'll haul away, Joe!
   But then I got a Brooklyn gal; she durn near drove me crazy.
   Chorus: Way, haul away, we'll haul away, Joe!

4. Way, haul away, we'll haul away together;
   Chorus: Way, haul away, we'll haul away, Joe!
   Way, haul away, we'll haul for better weather.
   Chorus: Way, haul away, we'll haul away, Joe!

Three Jolly Fishermen

A ridiculously proper song poking gentle fun at itself.

1. There were three jol-ly fish-er-men,_____ There were three jol-ly fish-er-men, Fish-er, fish-er, men-men-men,
2. The first one's name was A-bra-ham,_____ The first one's name was A-bra-ham, A-bra, A-bra, ham-ham-ham,

Fish-er, fish-er, men-men-men, There were three jol-ly fish-er-men.
A-bra, A-bra, ham-ham-ham, The first one's name was A-bra-ham.

3. The second one's name was Isaac,
The second one's name was Isaac,
I, I, zak-zak-zak,
I, I, zak-zak-zak,
The second one's name was Isaac.

4. The third one's name was Jacob,
The third one's name was Jacob,
Ja, Ja, cub-cub-cub,
Ja, Ja, cub-cub-cub,
The third one's name was Jacob.

5. They all sailed up to Jericho,
They all sailed up to Jericho,
Jerry, Jerry, co-co-co,
Jerry, Jerry, co-co-co,
They all sailed up to Jericho.

6. They wished they'd gone to Amsterdam,
They wished they'd gone to Amsterdam,
Amster, Amster, sh-sh-sh,
Amster, Amster, sh-sh-sh,
They wished they'd gone to Amsterdam.

7. You must not say that naughty word,
You must not say that naughty word,
Naughty, naughty, word-word-word,
Naughty, naughty, word-word-word,
You must not say that naughty word.

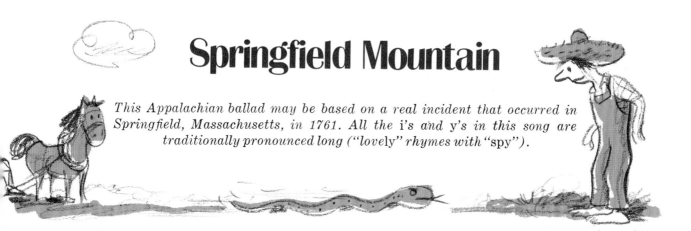

Springfield Mountain

This Appalachian ballad may be based on a real incident that occurred in Springfield, Massachusetts, in 1761. All the i's and y's in this song are traditionally pronounced long ("lovely" rhymes with "spy").

Mournfully

1. On Spring-field Moun-tain, there did dwell A love-ly youth, I knew him well- i -ell.
2. One day, this love - ly youth did go Down to the mea- dow for to mow-i -ow.

Chorus:

Too - roo - dee - noo, too - roo - dee - nay, Too - roo-dee- noo, too - roo-dee - nay.

3. He scarce had mow'd half 'round the field
   When a pizen sarpint bit his heel-i-eel.

   Chorus: Too-roo-dee-noo, too-roo-dee-nay,
   Too-roo-dee-noo, too-roo-dee-nay.

4. They took him home to Molly dear,
   For he did look so very queer-i-eer.

   Chorus

5. Now, Molly dear had ruby lips,
   With which the pizen she did sip-i-yip.

   Chorus

6. But Molly had a hollow tooth,
   And so the pizen killed them bo-i-oth.

   Chorus

Drill, Ye Tarriers, Drill

A unique case of social injustice is chronicled in this railroad song. Tarriers were unskilled Irish railroad workmen who were stationed beside the steam drills to remove loosened rock.

With a solid beat

1. Ev - 'ry mor - ning at sev - en o' - clock There were twen - ty tar - ri - ers a - work - in' at the rock, And the boss comes a - long and he says, "Keep still!" And come down heav - y on the cast - iron drill.

2. The boss was a fine man down to the ground, And he mar - ried a la - dy six feet round. She baked good bread and she baked it well, And she baked it hard as the holes of hell.

3. Now, our new foreman was Jim McCann.
   By God, he was a blamed mean man.
   Last week a premature blast went off
   And a mile in the air went big Jim Goff.
   Chorus

4. The next time payday came around,
   Jim Goff a dollar short was found.
   When asked what for, came this reply:
   "You was docked for the time you was up in the sky!"
   Chorus

Chorus: And drill, ye tarriers, drill;
    Drill, ye tarriers, drill;
    For it's work all day for the sugar in your tay,
    Down behind the railway,
    And drill, ye tarriers, drill,
    And blast and fire.

Tinga Layo

A calypso song from the West Indies often sung by groups in two parts.

Lilting

Chorus:

Ting - a Lay - o! Come, lit - tle don - key come. Ting- a

Lay - o! Come, lit - tle don - key come.

Fine

1. Me don - key walk, me don - key talk, Me don - key eat with a knife and fork.
2. Me don - key eat, me don - key sleep, Me don - key kick with his two hind feet.

D. C.

PART III
CLAPPING, SNAPPING, AND MAKING PECULIAR NOISES

Motion songs and wordplay songs

Miss Mary Mack

A well-known partner hand-clapping game with some new verses. Clapping pattern for each line: clap, slap, clap, right, clap, left, clap, both,* as indicated above the music.

1. Miss Ma-ry Mack, Mack, Mack, All dressed in black, black, black With sil-ver
moth-er, moth-er, moth-er For fif-ty cents, cents, cents To see the

buck-les, buck-les, buck-les, Up and down her back, back, back. 2. I asked my
ele-phant, ele-phant, ele-phant Jump the fence, fence, fence.

3. He jumped so high, high, high
He reached the sky, sky, sky
And didn't come back, back, back
Till the fourth of July, -ly, -ly.

4. Miss Betty Bean, Bean, Bean,
All dressed in green, green, green,
She never smiled, smiled, smiled,
She was too mean, mean, mean.

5. Miss Lucy Light, Light, Light,
All dressed in white, white, white,
She kicked her brother, brother, brother
Just out of spite, spite, spite.

6. Miss Dora Down, Down, Down,
All dressed in brown, brown, brown,
She pinched her sister, sister, sister
Just to make her frown, frown, frown.

7. Miss Flora Fay, Fay, Fay,
All dressed in gray, gray, gray
Had the mumps and measles, measles, measles
On a single day, day, day.

8. There's soda crackers, crackers, crackers
Up on the shelf, shelf, shelf;
If you want any more, more, more,
You can sing it yourself,-self, -self!

*clap—clap hands together
slap—slap hands on lap
right—clap your right hand against partner's right hand
left—clap your left hand against partner's left hand
both—clap both your hands against partner's two hands

Mary Ann McCarthy

A motion song to the tune of "The Battle Hymn of the Republic."

With gusto

Ma - ry Ann Mc- Car - thy went a - fish - ing for some clams,

Ma - ry Ann Mc- Car - thy went a - fish - ing for some clams,

Ma - ry Ann Mc- Car - thy went a - fish - ing for some clams, But she

The Old Navy

When this song is repeated the pantomime
may be accompanied by loud, warlike noises.

Oh, we don't have to march like the in-fan-try, Ride like the cav-al-ry,

Shoot like the ar-til-le-ry. We don't have to fly o-ver Ger-man-y.

We are the old Na-vy. We are the old Na-

vy, by gum! *(spoken)* We are the old Na - vy, by gum! *(spoken)* And

then, by gum, we'll all go to sea a- gain. We are the old Na - vy.

Suggested, for second time:

Oh, we don't have to (Hup! two, three, four!)
(Giddap, giddap, giddap, giddap!)
(Heh-heh-heh-heh-heh-heh-heh-heh-heh-heh-heh-heh!).
We don't have to (Zooooooooom!).
We are the old Navy.
etc.

Mammy Don't 'Low

Members of the group take turns suggesting activities that "Mammy don't 'low," which everybody cheerfully proceeds to perform, thus dramatizing the common fate of maternal interdictions everywhere.

Moving along

Mam-my don't 'low no pick-in' and sing-in' round here.

Mam-my don't 'low no pick-in' and sing-in' round here.

We don't care what Mam-my don't 'low, Gon-na pick and sing an-y-how.

Mam-my don't 'low no pick-in' and sing-in' round here.

Suggested activities: Hand-clapping, foot-stomping, nose-thumbing, finger-snapping, head-scratching, belly-rolling, toe-touching, head-shaking, hiccuping, snorting and snoring, sobbing and sighing, etc.

The Desperado

A tale of one of the noisiest bad guys in history. The "war whoop" at the end of each verse and the chorus is usually made the traditional "Indian war-whoop" way, with the hand covering and uncovering the mouth rapidly at the w sound, giving a "wah-wah-wah" effect.

Fast

C

1. He was a des-per-a-do from the wild and wool-ly West. He
2. He went to Co-ney Is-land, just to take in all the sights. He

G⁷

came in-to the ci-ty just to give the West a rest. He
saw the hoot-chie koot-chie and the girls all dressed in tights. He

C

wore a big som-bre-ro and a gun be-neath his vest, And
got so derned ex-ci-ted that he shot out all the lights, And

ev - 'ry - where he went he gave his w - w - w - war whoop.

Chorus:

He was a brave, bold man and a des - per - a - do, From

Crip - ple Creek, way down in Co - lo - ra - do, And he

walked a - round like a big tor - na - do, And
ev - 'ry - where he went he gave his w - w - w - war whoop.

wobble

3. A great big fat policeman was awalking down his beat.
   He saw this desperado come awalking down the street.
   He grabbed him by the whiskers and he grabbed him by the seat,
   And threw him where he wouldn't give his w-w-w-war whoop.

Chorus: He was a brave, bold man and a desperado,
   From Cripple Creek, way down in Colorado,
   And he walked around like a big tornado,
   And ev'rywhere he went he gave his w-w-w-war whoop.

Down by the Old Millstream

A version of an old American favorite that includes motions for most of the words in the song. It is fun to try singing only the few words without motions, substituting the appropriate motions for the other words, trying to end up all together.

Down by the old mill - stream, Where I first met you With your eyes so blue, Dressed in ging - ham too. It was there I knew, That you loved me true. You were six-

teen, _____ My vil-lage queen, _____ Down by the old mill - stream.

Motions:
Old—stroke an imaginary beard
Mill—make a rotary motion with one hand
Stream—make ripplelike motions with hands
First—hold up one finger
Met—shake imaginary hand
You—point to someone
Eyes—shade eyes with hand
So—make sewing motion with hands
Blue—point to something blue, or to sky
Gingham—make imaginary crisscross lines on your
    chest
Too—hold up two fingers
Knew—point to temple
You—point to someone else
Loved—put hand on heart and make a stupid, sentimental
    face
Me—point to self
True—hold up right hand as if taking an oath
Sixteen—hold up eight fingers twice
Queen—hold fingertips above head to form imaginary
    crown

Another favorite version of this song adds opposites to some words in each
line, as below. The additional words are sung on the same note as the
immediately preceding word—except the final phrase, which is dragged out
to the tune of the equivalent phrase of "How Dry I Am."

Down by the old (not the new but the old) millstream (not the river but the stream),
Where I first (not last but first) met you (not me but you),
With your eyes (not ears but eyes) so blue (not green but blue),
Dressed in gingham (not calico but gingham) too (not three but too).
It was there (not here but there) I knew (not old but knew),
That I loved (not hated but loved) you true (not false but true).
You were sixteen (not fifteen but sixteen),
My village queen (not the king but the queen),
Down by the old (not the new but the old) millstream (not the river but the stream).

The Story the Crow Told Me

For those who have an irresistible urge to caw,
here is a deeply satisfying song.

1. Now, if you will lis- ten, I'll sing you a song. It's aw - ful fun - ny, but it
2. My gal took sick the oth - er day. The doc - tor said she's gon- na

won't take long, All a - bout a crow in a hick- o - ry tree,
pass a - way. I bought her a gir- dle at the dry - goods store.

One lit - tle sto - ry that the crow told me.
She's in bet - ter shape than she was be - fore.

Chorus:

(cawing sounds) One lit - tle sto - ry that the crow told me

(cawing sounds) In a hick - o - ry tree.

3. Now there was an owl, lived up in an oak.
   The more he heard the less he spoke,
   And the less he spoke the more he heard.
   Why aren't we like that wise old bird?

   Chorus: (*Cawing sounds*)
   One little story that the crow told me
   (*Cawing sounds*)
   In a hickory tree.

4. I was in my garden a-pickin' peas.
   I thought I heard a little chicken sneeze,
   Sneezin' so hard with the whooping cough,
   Sneezed his head and his tail right off.

   Chorus

KERCHOO!

Billy Magee Magaw

A raucous and rollicking version of the mournful folk ballad "The Three Ravens." At the "Caw! Caw! Caw!" all singers flap their arms three times in time to the music. The tune is almost identical to that of "When Johnny Comes Marching Home."

1. There were three crows sat on a tree, Oh, Bil - ly Ma - gee Ma - gaw; ___ There
2. Said one old crow un - to his mate, Said

were three crows sat on a tree, Oh, Bil - ly Ma - gee Ma - gaw; ___ There
one old crow un - to his mate, Said

were three crows sat on a tree, And they were black as crows could be,
one old crow un - to his mate, "What shall we do for grub to ate?" And they

all flapped their wings and cried, "Caw! Caw! Caw!

Bil - ly Ma - gee Ma - gaw!" ___ And they all flapped their wings and cried,

"Bil - ly Ma - gee Ma - gaw!" ___

3. "There lies a horse on yonder plain,
   Oh, Billy Magee Magaw;
   There lies a horse on yonder plain,
   Oh, Billy Magee Magaw;
   There lies a horse on yonder plain
   Who's by some cruel butcher slain,"
   And they all flapped their wings and cried,
   "Caw! Caw! Caw! Billy Magee Magaw!"
   And they all flapped their wings and cried,
   "Billy Magee Magaw!"

4. "We'll perch ourselves on his backbone,
   Oh, Billy Magee Magaw;
   We'll perch ourselves on his backbone,
   Oh, Billy Magee Magaw;
   We'll perch ourselves on his backbone
   And pick his eyes out one by one,"
   And they all flapped their wings and cried,
   "Caw! Caw! Caw! Billy Magee Magaw!"
   And they all flapped their wings and cried,
   "Billy Magee Magaw!"

5. "The meat we'll eat before it's stale,
   Oh Billy Magee Magaw;
   The meat we'll eat before it's stale,
   Oh Billy Magee Magaw;
   The meat we'll eat before it's stale,
   Till nothing's left but bones and tail,"
   And they all flapped their wings and cried,
   "Caw! Caw! Caw! Billy Magee Magaw!"
   And they all flapped their wings and cried,
   "Billy Magee Magaw!"

The Bear Went Over the Mountain

An old song with a surprise ending.

3. He climbed the other mountain,
   He climbed the other mountain,
   He climbed the other mountain,
   And what do you think he saw?

   Chorus 1: And what do you think he saw?
   (blood-curdling shriek)
   And what do you think he saw?
   (blood-curdling shriek)

4. He saw another mountain,
   He saw another mountain,
   He saw another mountain,
   And what do you think he did?

   Chorus 2: And what do you think he did?
   (blood-curdling shriek)
   And what do you think he did?
   (blood-curdling shriek)

5. He climbed the other mountain,
   He climbed the other mountain,
   He climbed the other mountain,
   And what do you think he saw?

   Chorus 1

6. He saw another mountain,
   He saw another mountain,
   He saw another mountain,
   And what do you think he did?

   Chorus 2

   Spoken: He dropped dead from
   climbing so many mountains!

72

PART IV
QUESTIONS AND ANSWERS

*"He-and-she" songs, and other songs that divide
a group into two parts*

A Hole in the Bucket

For an amusing effect, let the boys sing the "she" parts in a sweet and timid
manner, while the girls sing the "he" parts as harshly and bossily as they can.

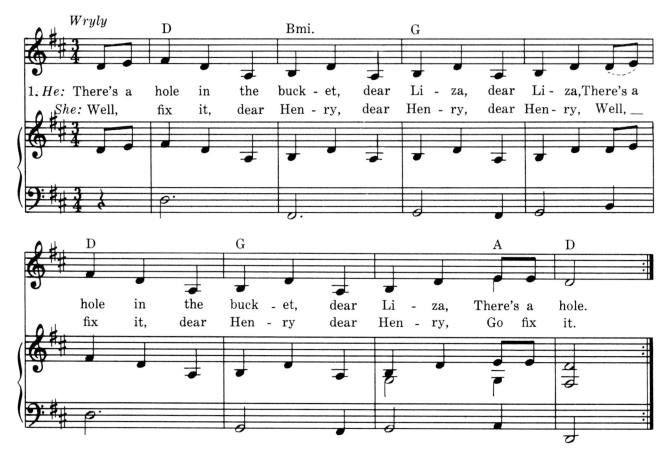

2. *He:*
   With what shall I fix it, dear Liza, dear Liza,
   With what shall I fix it, dear Liza, with what?
   She:
   With a straw, dear Henry, dear Henry, dear Henry,
   With a straw, dear Henry, dear Henry, with a straw.

3. *He:*
   But the straw is too long, dear Liza, dear Liza,
   But the straw is too long, dear Liza, too long.
   She:
   Then cut it, dear Henry, dear Henry, dear Henry,
   Then cut it, dear Henry, dear Henry, then cut it.

4. *He:*
   Well, how shall I cut it, dear Liza, dear Liza,
   Well, how shall I cut it, dear Liza, well, how?
   She:
   With a knife, dear Henry, dear Henry, dear Henry,
   With a knife, dear Henry, dear Henry, with a knife.

5. *He:*
   But the knife is too dull, dear Liza, dear Liza,
   But the knife is too dull, dear Liza, too dull.
   She:
   Then sharpen it, dear Henry, dear Henry, dear Henry,
   Then sharpen it, dear Henry, dear Henry, then sharpen it.

6. *He:*
   With what shall I sharpen it, dear Liza, dear Liza,
   With what shall I sharpen it, dear Liza, with what?
   She:
   With a whetstone, dear Henry, dear Henry, dear Henry,
   With a whetstone, dear Henry, dear Henry, with a whetstone.

7. *He:*
   But the whetstone's too dry, dear Liza, dear Liza,
   But the whetstone's too dry, dear Liza, too dry.
   She:
   Then wet it, dear Henry, dear Henry, dear Henry,
   Then wet it, dear Henry, dear Henry, then wet it.

8. *He:*
   With what shall I wet it, dear Liza, dear Liza,
   With what shall I wet it, dear Liza, with what?
   She:
   With water, dear Henry, dear Henry, dear Henry,
   With water, dear Henry, dear Henry, with water.

9. *He:*
   Well, how shall I carry it, dear Liza, dear Liza,
   Well, how shall I carry it, dear Liza, well, how?
   She:
   In a bucket, dear Henry, dear Henry, dear Henry,
   In a bucket, dear Henry, dear Henry, in a bucket.

10. *He:*
   BUT THERE'S A HOLE IN THE BUCKET, DEAR LIZA, DEAR LIZA,
   THERE'S A HOLE IN THE BUCKET, DEAR LIZA, A HOLE.

The Deaf Woman's Courtship

One half of the group sings the questions in an energetic way, and the other half sings back the answers in a quavery, old-ladyish manner, until the final verse. Then the "old women" sing the final line as loudly and triumphantly as they can.

Nattering and chattering

1. *He:* Old wo - man, old wo - man, will you do my wash - ing?
2. *He:* Old wo - man, old wo - man, will you do my iron - ing?

She: Speak a lit - tle loud - er, sir; I'm rath - er hard of hear - ing.

3. *He:*   Old woman, old woman, will you do my darning?
           Old woman, old woman, will you do my darning?
  She: Speak a little louder, sir; I'm rather hard of hearing.
           Speak a little louder, sir; I'm rather hard of hearing.

4. *He:*   Old woman, old woman, can I come acourting?
           Old woman, old woman, can I come acourting?
  She: Speak a little louder sir; I think I almost heard you.
           Speak a little louder sir; I think I almost heard you.

5. *He:*   Old woman, old woman, marry me tomorrow.
           Old woman, old woman, marry me tomorrow.
  She: GOODNESS GRACIOUS MERCY SAKES! NOW I REALLY
           HEARD YOU!
           GOODNESS GRACIOUS MERCY SAKES! NOW I REALLY
           HEARD YOU!

Daughters, Will You Marry?

Music wins a rare victory over the respectable professions of medicine, teaching, and law in this question-and-answer song.

Moving along

1. *Boys:* Daugh - ters, will you mar - ry? *Girls:* Yea, Fa - ther, yea.
2. *Boys:* Daugh - ters, will you mar - ry? *Girls:* Yea, Fa - ther, yea.

Boys: Will you mar-ry a doc - tor? *Girls:* Nay, Fa - ther, nay.
Boys: Will you mar-ry a law - yer? *Girls:* Nay, Fa - ther, nay.

F   B♭   C⁷   F

doc - tor's wife   I   will   not   be;   Tor - tu - ring peo-ple is   not   for me.
law - yer's wife   I   will   not   be;   Cheat - ing peo-ple is   not   for me.

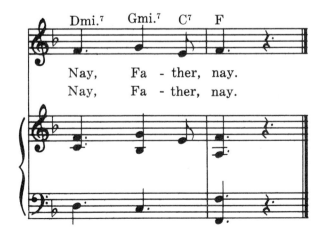

Dmi.⁷   Gmi.⁷   C⁷   F

Nay,   Fa - ther, nay.
Nay,   Fa - ther, nay.

3. **Boys:** Daughters, will you marry?
    Girls: Yea, Father, yea.
    Boys: Will you marry a teacher?
    Girls: Nay, Father, nay.
         A teacher's wife I will not be;
         Punishing children is not for me.
         Nay, Father, nay.

4. **Boys:** Daughters, will you marry?
    Girls: Yea, Father, yea.
    Boys: Will you marry a fiddler?
    Girls: Yea, Father, yea.
         I'd like to be a fiddler's wife,
         Singing and dancing all my life.
         Yea, Father, yea.

Paper of Pins

A song with a twist at the end.

Lilting

1. *Boys:* I'll give to you a pa-per of pins, For that is how my love be-gins, If
Girls: I won't ac-cept your pa-per of pins, If that is how your love be-gins, And

you will mar-ry me, me, me, If you will mar-ry me.
I won't mar-ry you, you, you, And I won't mar-ry you.

2. *Boys:* I'll give to you a dress of red,
All trimmed around with golden thread,
If you will marry me, me, me,
If you will marry me.

   Girls: I won't accept your dress of red,
All trimmed around with golden thread,
And I won't marry you, you, you,
And I won't marry you.

3. *Boys:* I'll give to you the key to my heart,
That we may love and never part,
If you will marry me, me, me,
If you will marry me.

   Girls: I won't accept the key to your heart,
That we may love and never part,
And I won't marry you, you, you,
And I won't marry you.

4. *Boys:* I'll give to you the key to my chest,
With all the money I possess,
If you will marry me, me, me,
If you will marry me.

   Girls: I *will* accept the key to your chest,
With all the money you possess.
Yes, I will marry you, you, you,
Yes, I will marry you.

5. *Boys:* (*triumphantly*)
Ha ha ha, it's very funny,
You don't love me but you love my money.
Well, I *won't* marry you, you, you,
Now *I* won't marry *you*!

Where Are You Going, My Pretty Maid?

A presumptuous suitor gets his comeuppance in this old English folk song.

3. *He:* What is your fortune, my pretty maid?
   What is your fortune, my pretty maid?

   She: "My face is my fortune, sir," she said, "sir" she said, "sir," she said;
   "My face is my fortune, sir," she said.

4. *He:* Then I can't marry you, my pretty maid!
   Then I can't marry you, my pretty maid!

   She: "Nobody asked you, sir," she said, "sir," she said, "sir," she said,
   "Nobody asked you, sir!" she said.

Soldier, Soldier

A question-and-answer song going back to Reconstruction days.

Snappy

1. *She:* Sol - dier, sol-dier, will you mar - ry me now, With your mus - ket, fife, and drum? *He:* How can I mar-ry such a pret- ty lit -tle thing When I

have no coat to put on, on, When I have no coat to put

on? *All:* So she ran and she ran to her grand-fa-ther's chest As

fast as she could run, And she found him a coat of the
A⁷

ver - y, ver - y best, And the sol - dier put it on, on, And the
G   D   A⁷

sol - dier put it on.
A⁷   D

2. *She:* Soldier, soldier, will you marry me now,
With your musket, fife, and drum?

He: How can I marry such a pretty little thing
When I have no hat to put on, on,
When I have no hat to put on?

All: So she ran and she ran to her grandfather's chest
As fast as she could run,
And she found him a hat of the very, very best,
And the soldier put it on, on,
And the soldier put it on.

3. *She:*   Soldier, soldier, will you marry me now,
            With your musket, fife, and drum?

   He: How can I marry such a pretty little thing
            When I have no gloves to put on, on,
            When I have no gloves to put on?

   All: So she ran and she ran to her grandfather's chest,
            As fast as she could run,
            And she found him some gloves of the very, very best,
            And the soldier put them on, on,
            And the soldier put them on.

4. *She:*   Soldier, soldier, will you marry me now,
            With your musket, fife, and drum?

   He: How can I marry such a pretty little thing
            When I have no boots to put on, on,
            When I have no boots to put on?

   All: So she ran and she ran to her grandfather's chest
            As fast as she could run,
            And she found him some boots of the very, very best,
            And the soldier put them on, on,
            And the soldier put them on.

5. *She:*   Soldier, soldier, will you marry me now,
            With your musket, fife, and drum?

   He: How can I marry such a pretty little thing
            With a wife and a baby at home, home,
            With a wife and a baby at home?

Oh, Won't You Sit Down?

This old Negro camp-meeting song is most effective when sung in two parts,
with one part of the group singing the questions and the other the answers.

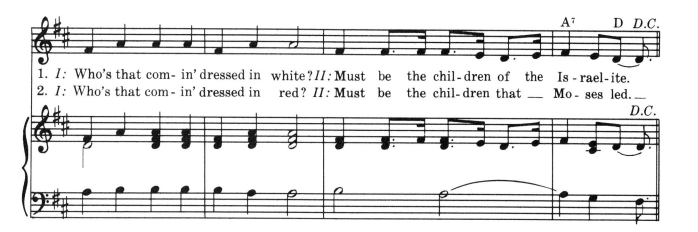

1. I: Who's that com- in' dressed in white? II: Must be the chil- dren of the Is - rael- ite.
2. I: Who's that com- in' dressed in red? II: Must be the chil- dren that __ Mo- ses led. __

3. *Group I:* Who's that comin' dressed in black?
   Group II: Must be the hypocrites turning back.

   Chorus: I: Oh, won't you sit down?
   II: Lawd, I can't sit down.
   I: Oh, won't you sit down?
   II: Lawd, I can't sit down.
   I: Oh, won't you sit down?
   II: Lawd, I can't sit down.
   I just got to heaven, got to look around.

The Keeper

A song that may go back to the days of Robin Hood, when keepers, or game wardens, were employed both to guard the King's preserves from poachers and to kill game for the royal table.

Rollicking

All: The keep-er would a - hun-ting go, And un-der his cloak he car-ried a bow,

All for to shoot at a mer-ry lit - tle doe, A-mong the leaves so - green, O.

Chorus:

Voice I: *Voice II:*
Jack- ie   boy?   Mas - ter? *I:* Sing ye well? *II:* Ve- ry well. *I:* Hey down, *II:* Ho   down,

Both: Der-ry der-ry down, A-mong the leaves so ___ green, O. **I:** To my hey down down, To my ho down down, **I:** Hey down, **II:** Ho down,

Both: Der-ry der-ry down, A-mong the leaves so ___ green, O.

2. *All:* The first doe he shot at he missed.
    The second doe he trimmed he kissed.
    The third doe went where nobody wist,
    Among the leaves so green, O.   *Chorus*

3. *All:* The fourth doe she did cross the plain;
    The keeper fetched her back again.
    Where she is now she may remain,
    Among the leaves so green, O.   *Chorus*

4. *All:* The fifth doe she did cross the brook;
    The keeper fetched her back with his crook.
    Where she is now you must go look,
    Among the leaves so green, O.   *Chorus*

Chorus: *Voice I:* Jackie boy?
        Voice II: Master?
          I: Sing ye well?
         II: Very well.
          I: Hey down,
         II: Ho down,
      Both: Derry derry down,
               Among the leaves so green, O.
          I: To my hey down down,
         II: To my ho down down,
          I: Hey down,
         II: Ho down,
      Both: Derry, derry down,
               Among the leaves so green, O.

Buffalo Boy

Another promising courtship hits the dust in this old American question-and-answer folk song. It is fun to reverse roles in this song and let the boys sing the "she" verses in as high and squeaky voices as they can muster.

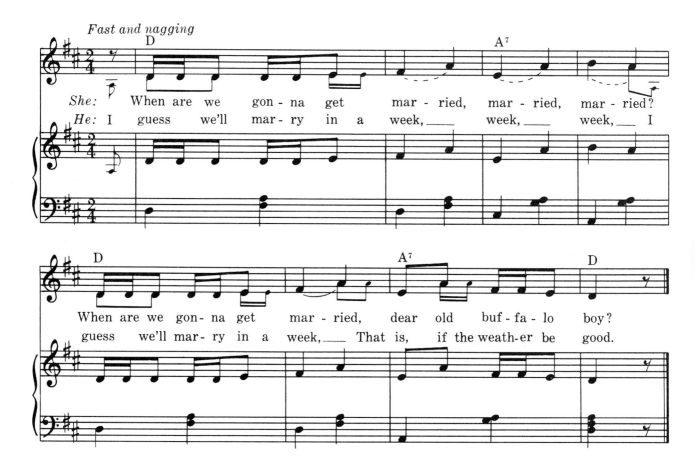

Fast and nagging

She: When are we gon - na get mar - ried, mar - ried, mar - ried?
He: I guess we'll mar - ry in a week,___ week,___ week,___ I

When are we gon - na get mar - ried, dear old buf - fa - lo boy?
guess we'll mar - ry in a week,___ That is, if the weath-er be good.

2. *She:* How will you come to the wedding, wedding, wedding,
How will you come to the wedding, dear old buffalo boy?

   He: I guess I'll come in my oxcart, oxcart, oxcart,
I guess I'll come in my oxcart, that is, if the weather be good.

3. *She:* Why don't you come in your buggy, buggy, buggy,
Why don't you come in your buggy, dear old buffalo boy?

   He: My ox won't fit in my buggy, buggy, buggy,
My ox won't fit in my buggy, not even if the weather be good.

4. *She:* Who will you bring to the wedding, wedding, wedding,
Who will you bring to the wedding, dear old buffalo boy?

   He: I guess I'll bring my children, children, children,
I guess I'll bring my children, that is, if the weather be good.

5. *She:* I didn't know you had children, children, children,
I didn't know you had children, dear old buffalo boy.

   He: Oh, yes, I have five children, children, children,
Oh, yes, I have five children, six if the weather be good.

6. *She:* There ain't gonna be no wedding, wedding, wedding,
There ain't gonna be no wedding, not even if the weather be good!

PART V
SPUR OF THE MOMENT

*Songs with words, verses, and motions
to be improvised on the spot*

If I Had the Wings of a Turtledove

An improvising game song. Members of the group take turns providing a place and a person or group of persons to go with it, as in the examples given here. The whole group choruses the sarcastic asides in each verse and joins in the chorus.

1. If I had the wings of a tur-tle-dove, *Caterpillar!*
2. If I had the wings of a tur-tle-dove, *Caterpillar!*

Back to our camp I would fly. *I'd crawl!* And
Back to Mount Ev-'rest I'd fly, *I'd crawl!* And

there I would play with those coun-se-lors, *Good gravy!* And
there I would play with the Abomina-ble Snowman, *Good gravy!* And

there I would play till I die.

(spoken) Boo - hoo!

Chorus: G

Sing too - ra - lie - oo - ra - lie - oo - ra - lie   (spoken) Re - peat!   Sing

too - ra - lie - oo - ra - lie - aye.   (spoken) Once more!   Sing -

C ... **G** *(spoken)*

too - ra - lie - oo - ra - lie - oo - ra - lie; And in conclusion! Sing

D⁷ ... **G**

too - ra - lie - oo - ra - lie - aye.

3. If I had the wings of a turtledove (*Spoken:* Caterpillar!)
Back to the South Pole I'd fly. (*Spoken:* I'd crawl!)
And there I would play with those penguins (*Spoken:* Good gravy!)
And there I would play till I die. (*Spoken:* Boo hoo!)

Chorus: Sing too-ra-lie-oo-ra-lie-oo-ra-lie (*Spoken:* Repeat!)
Sing too-ra-lie-oo-ra-lie-aye; (*Spoken:* Once more!)
Sing too-ra-lie-oo-ra-lie-oo-ra-lie (*Spoken:* And in conclusion!)
Sing too-ra-lie-oo-ra-lie-aye.

4. If I had the wings of a turtledove (Caterpillar!)
Back to our kitchen I'd fly. (I'd crawl!)
And there I would play with those cockroaches (Good gravy!)
And there I would play till I die. (Boo hoo!)

Chorus

5. If I had the wings of a turtledove (Caterpillar!)
Back to Australia I'd fly. (I'd crawl!)
And there I would play with the koala bears (Good gravy!)
And there I would play till I die. (Boo hoo!)

Chorus

etc.

Oh, You Can't Get to Heaven

*The possibilities for new verses of this echo song
are legion, and rhyming is not absolutely necessary.*

1. Oh, you can't get to heav-en (Oh, you can't get to heav-en) On rol-ler skates (On rol-ler skates),'Cause you'd roll right by ('Cause you'd roll right by) Those pear-ly gates (Those pear-ly

gates) Oh, you can't get to hea-ven on rol-ler skates,'Cause you'd roll right

by those pear-ly gates. I ain't gon-na grieve _____ my Lord no more. _____

2. Oh, you can't get to heaven (Oh, you can't get to heaven)
   In a rocking chair (In a rocking chair),
   'Cause the Lord don't want ('Cause the Lord don't want)
   No lazybones there (No lazybones there).
   Oh, you can't get to heaven in a rocking chair,
   'Cause the Lord don't want no lazybones there.
   I ain't gonna grieve my Lord no more.

Chorus: I ain't gonna grieve my Lord no more,
I ain't gonna grieve my Lord no more,
I ain't gonna grieve my Lord no more.

Chorus 3. Oh, you can't get to heaven (Oh, you can't get to heaven)
In a limousine (In a limousine),
'Cause the Lord don't sell ('Cause the Lord don't sell)
No gasoline (no gasoline).
Oh, you can't get to heaven in a limousine,
'Cause the Lord don't sell no gasoline.
I ain't gonna grieve my Lord no more.

Chorus 4. Oh, you can't get to heaven (Oh, you can't get to heaven)
In a motorcar (In a motorcar),
'Cause a motorcar ('Cause a motorcar)
Won't go that far (Won't go that far).
Oh, you can't get to heaven in a motorcar,
'Cause a motorcar won't go that far.
I ain't gonna grieve my Lord no more.

Chorus 5. Oh, you can't get to heaven (Oh, you can't get to heaven)
In a birch canoe (In a birch canoe);
You'd need to paddle (You'd need to paddle)
Till you're black and blue (Till you're black and blue).
Oh, you can't get to heaven in a birch canoe;
You'd need to paddle till you're black and blue,
I ain't gonna grieve my Lord no more.

Chorus—faster:

I ain't gon-na grieve my Lord no more, I ain't gon-na grieve my Lord no more, I ain't gon-na grieve my Lord no more.

Chorus 6. If you get there (If you get there)
Before I do (Before I do),
Just dig a hole (Just dig a hole)
And pull me through (And pull me through).
If you get there before I do,
Just dig a hole and pull me through.
I ain't gonna grieve my Lord no more.

Chorus 7. There's one more thing (There's one more thing)
I ought to tell (I ought to tell):
If you don't go to heaven (If you don't go to heaven)
You'll go to hell (You'll go to hell).
There's one more thing I ought to tell:
If you don't go to heaven you'll go to hell.
I ain't gonna grieve my Lord no more.

Chorus 8. There's bread and cheese (There's bread and cheese)
Upon the shelf (Upon the shelf);
If you want any more (If you want any more),
You can get it yourself (You can get it yourself).
There's bread and cheese upon the shelf;
If you want any more you can get it yourself.
I ain't gonna grieve my Lord no more.

Roll, Jordan, Roll

Everyone has a chance to give a serious, or preferably absurd, reason why he will or will not be there to see old Jordan roll in this cheerful spiritual that begins with almost the same tune as the chorus of "The Camptown Races." Included here are some answers given during a beach picnic on Cape Cod.

Chorus: Roll, Jordan, roll,
Roll, Jordan, roll,
I want to go to heaven when I die
To see old Jordan roll.

3. Oh, Sam (the name of one of the group), will you be there?
I have to ask my mommy.
Oh, sitting on a kingdom to see old Jordan roll.

4. **Roger:**   Only if Helen isn't going.

G   (spoken)   (sung)

1. Oh,   Mary,   will   you   be   there?   (Mary) Only if they have marsh-
mallow ripple ice cream.   Oh,

2. Oh,   Kathy,   will   you   be   there? (Kathy) Not if I can help it.

D⁷   G

sit - ting   on   a   king - dom   to   see   old   Jor - dan   roll.

5. Helen: Only if I can go with Roger.

6. Artie: No.

7. Debbie: Do they let you go skinny-dipping?

8. Hank: I'd rather go to the movies.

9. Pablo: You'll have to check with my social secretary.

My Gal's a Corker

*More verses can be invented to describe
other features of this all-American beauty.*

My gal's a cor - ker; she's a New Yor - ker.

I'll buy her an - y - thing to keep her in style.

1. She's got a pair of legs just like two whis - key kegs.
2. She's got a pair of lips just like po - ta - to chips.

Hot dog, that's where my mon-ey goes! _____

last time

3. My gal's a corker; she's a New Yorker.
   I'll buy her anything to keep her in style.
   She's got a pair of eyes just like two custard pies.
   Hot dog, that's where my money goes!

4. She's got a pair of hips like two battleships. . . .

5. She's got a big red nose just like a cabbage rose. . . .

6. She's got a pointy chin just like a safety pin. . . .

7. She's got a head of hair just like a grizzly bear. . . .

The Limerick Song

Aye-aye-aye-aye

Here is a song that can go on for hours, with all members
of the group adding their favorite limericks—if they dare!

Chorus:

Aye - aye - aye-aye, _____ In Chi - na they

nev - er grow chil - ly. _____ So sing me an - oth - er verse that's

worse than the first verse; Make sure that it's fool - ish and sil - ly. _____

1. A tutor who tooted the flute, _____ Tried to tutor two tooters to toot. _____ Said the two to the tutor, "Is it tougher to toot, or To tutor two tooters to toot?" _____

2. There was an old man from Peru _____ Who dreamed he was eating his shoe. _____ When he woke in a fright In the _ dark of the night, _ He found it was perfectly true. _____

3. There once was a man from Calcutta
   Who spoke with a terrible stutter;
   At breakfast he said,
   "Give me b-b-b-bread
   And b-b-b-b-b-butter."

   Chorus: Aye-aye-aye-aye,
   In China they never grow chilly.
   So sing me another verse that's worse
      than the first verse;
   Make sure that it's foolish and silly.

4. There was a young fellow of Perth
   Who was born on the day of his birth;
   He was married, they say,
   On his wife's wedding day,
   And he died when he quitted the earth.

   Chorus

5. A man who was dining at Crewe
   Found quite a large mouse in his stew;
   Said the waiter, "Don't shout
   And wave it about,
   Or the rest will be wanting one too!"

   Chorus

Throw It Out the Window

Thinking of new verses for this song can become an addiction. Almost any song that can possibly be squeezed into the tune will turn out funny when it is given this new ending.

1. Old Moth-er Hub-bard __ went to the cup-board To fetch her poor dog a
2. Old __ King Cole was a mer-ry old soul, And a mer-ry old soul was

bone. _____ But when she got there, the cup-board was bare, So she
he, _____ He called for his pipe, and he called for his bowl, And __

Raucously

threw it out the win-dow, the win-dow, the sec-ond sto-ry win-dow;
threw them out the win-dow, the win-dow, the sec-ond sto-ry win-dow,

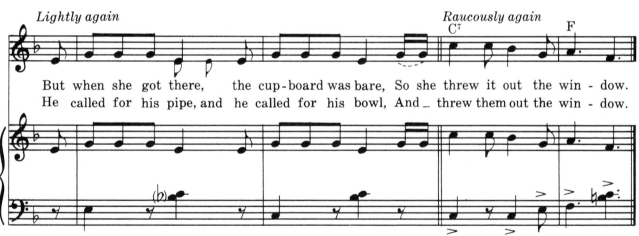

Lightly again

Raucously again

C⁷   F

But when she got there,   the cup-board was bare, So she threw it out the win - dow.
He called for his pipe, and he called for his bowl, And _ threw them out the win - dow.

3. Little Bo Peep has lost her sheep,
And doesn't know where to find them.
But leave them alone; when they come home
She'll throw them out the window,
The window, the second-story window;
But leave them alone; when they come home,
She'll throw them out the window.

4. Oh, where, oh, where has my little dog gone?
Oh, where, oh, where can he be?
With his ears cut short and his tail cut long,
I'll throw him out the window,
The window, the second-story window;
With his ears cut short and his tail cut long,
I'll throw him out the window.

5. Yankee Doodle went to town
Ariding on a pony;
He stuck a feather in his cap
And threw it out the window,
The window, the second-story window;
He stuck a feather in his cap,
And threw it out the window.

6. A-tisket, A-tasket,
A green and yellow basket,
I wrote a letter to my love
And threw it out the window,
The window, the second-story window;
I wrote a letter to my love
And threw it out the window.

ad infinitum

Two Little Blackbirds

To make up new verses for this song, think of a pair of opposites for the blackbirds' names. Then find a noun rhyming with the second opposite to designate where the blackbirds sit. For instance, blackbirds named Love *and* Hate *sit on a* gate.

With a light bounce

1. Two lit-tle black-birds sit-ting on a hill,
2. Two lit-tle black-birds sit-ting on a gate,

One named Jack and the oth-er named Jill.
One named Love and the oth-er named Hate.

3. Two little blackbirds sitting on a stick,
One named Healthy and the other named Sick.
Fly away, Healthy; fly away, Sick.
Come back, Healthy; come back, Sick.

4. Two little blackbirds sitting on a cloud,
One named Quiet and the other named Loud.
Fly away, Quiet; fly away, Loud.
Come back, Quiet; come back, Loud.

Fly a - way, Jack; fly a - way, Jill.
Fly a - way, Love; fly a - way, Hate.

Emi. **G⁷** **C**

Come back, Jack; come back, Jill.
Come back, Love; come back, Hate.

5. Two little blackbirds sitting on a kite,
One named Heavy and the other named Light.
Fly away, Heavy; fly away, Light.
Come back, Heavy; come back, Light.

(Last verse)
Two little blackbirds sitting on the bend;
That was the Beginning and this is the End.
Fly away, Beginning; fly away, End.
Come back, Beginning; come back, End.

The Kangaroo

A nonsense song (a corruption of the English ballad "The Carrion Crow")
that lends itself well to group improvisation. Members of the group take
turns thinking up places upon which the kangaroo sits to watch a tailor
or sailor perform some action (the sillier the better) that rhymes with the
place, as in the examples below.

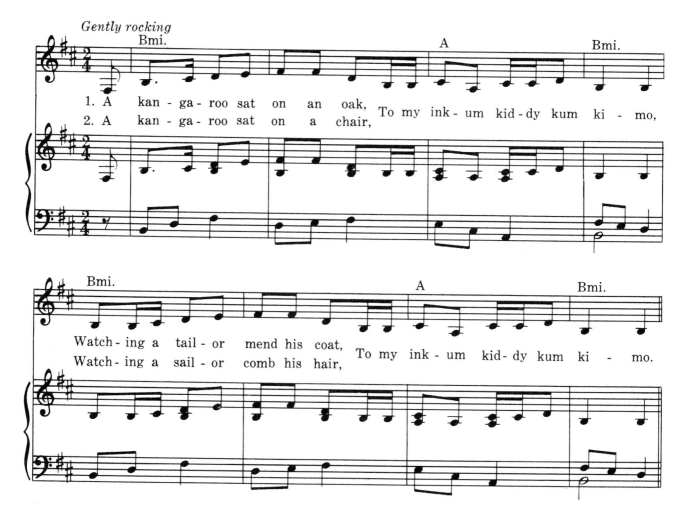

Gently rocking

1. A kan-ga-roo sat on an oak, To my ink-um kid-dy kum ki-mo,
2. A kan-ga-roo sat on a chair,

Watch-ing a tail-or mend his coat, To my ink-um kid-dy kum ki-mo.
Watch-ing a sail-or comb his hair,

3. A kangaroo sat on a bus,
   To my ink-um kiddy kum ki-mo,
   Watching a sailor make a fuss,
   To my ink-um kiddy kum ki-mo.

   Chorus: Ki-ma-nee-ro kiddy kum kee-ro,
           Ki-ma-nee-ro ki-me,
           Ba-ba-ba-ba billy illy ink-um,
           Ink-um kiddy kum ki-mo.

4. A kangaroo sat on a path,
   To my ink-um kiddy kum ki-mo,
   Watching a tailor take a bath,
   To my ink-um kiddy kum ki-mo.

   Chorus

Keemo Kyemo

A song from the Southern Appalachians with one of the most elaborate non-sense choruses in folk literature. Many simple doggerel or nonsense couplets can be improvised to fit between the lines of refrain. The original folk song is given below, followed by some verses improvised at a camp song-swapping session.

Chorus:

F

Kee - mo kye - mo dell - way hi - ho **Gmi.** Rum - pet - tee rump **C**

F Per - i - win - kle soap fat **C⁷** Link - horn nip cat **F** Hit 'em with a brick - bat

F Sing song kit - ty catch-ee **Dmi.** kye - **C⁷** me - **F** oh.

3. I love coffee, I love tea,
   Refrain: Sing-song kitty catch-ee kye-me-oh.
   I love the boys and the boys love me,
   Refrain: Sing-song kitty catch-ee kye-me-oh.

   Chorus: Kee-mo kye-mo dell-way
   Hi-ho rump-et-tee rump
   Periwinkle soap fat
   Link-horn nip cat
   Hit 'em with a brickbat
   Sing-song kitty catch-ee kye-me-oh.

4. Roses are red, violets are blue; (*refrain*)
   Sugar is sweet and so are you (*refrain*).

   Chorus

5. I see England, I see France; (*refrain*)
   I see Mary's polka-dot pants (*refrain*).

   Chorus

6. There was a man and he was rich; (*refrain*)
   He got a rash and began to itch (*refrain*).

   Chorus

Cape Cod Girls

An old New England sea shanty with some new verses.
Make up some more, following the pattern given.

Saltily
C

1. Cape Cod girls they have no combs, Heave a - way, heave a - way. They
2. Cape Cod girls they have no sleds, Heave a - way, heave a - way. They

comb their hair with cod - fish bones. We are bound for Aus - tra - lia.
slide down - hill on cod - fish heads. We are bound for Aus - tra - lia.

Chorus:

Heave ____ a - way, ____ my bul - ly bul - ly boys, heave a -

way;   Heave a - way,   Heave ___ a - way, ___ my

bul - ly bul - ly boys,   We   are   bound for   Aus - tra - lia.

3. Cape Cod cats they have no tails,
   Heave away, heave away;
   They blow away in heavy gales.
   We are bound for Australia.

   Chorus: Heave away, my bully bully boys,
              Heave away, heave away;
              Heave away, my bully bully boys,
              We are bound for Australia.

4. Cape Cod cars they have no wheels,
   Heave away, heave away;
   They ride along on slippery eels,
   We are bound for Australia.

   Chorus

5. Cape Cod kids don't wash no dishes,
   Heave away, heave away;
   They throw them after flying fishes,
   We are bound for Australia.

   Chorus

Polly Wolly Doodle

A popular minstrel song that invites new spur-of-the-moment verses, the sillier the better.

1. Oh, I went down South for to see my Sal, Sing
2. Oh, a grass-hop-per sit-tin' on a rail road track, Sing

Pol-ly wol-ly doo-dle all the day. My
Pol-ly wol-ly doo-dle all the day, Just

Sal she am a spun-ky gal, Sing
pick-in' his teeth with a car-pet tack, Sing

Pol-ly wol-ly doo-dle all the day.
Pol-ly wol-ly doo-dle all the day.

Chorus:

Fare thee well, ___ fare thee well, ___ Fare thee well, my fai - ry fay, For I'm goin' to Lu - zi - an - a For to see my Su - zi - an - na, Sing Pol - ly wol - ly doo - dle all day. _____

3. Oh, Pepsi-Cola is a drink,
   Sing Polly wolly doodle all day,
   That looks like water, and it tastes like ink,
   Sing Polly wolly doodle all the day.

   Chorus: Fare thee well, fare thee well,
       Fare thee well my fairy fay,
       For I'm goin' to Louziana
       For to see my Suzianna,
       Sing Polly wolly doodle all day.

4. I had a gal, she was six feet tall,
   Sing Polly wolly doodle all day;
   Slept in the kitchen with her feet in the hall,
   Sing Polly wolly doodle all the day.

   Chorus

5. Behind the barn, down on my knees,
   Sing Polly wolly doodle all day,
   I thought I heard a chicken sneeze,
   Sing Polly wolly doodle all the day.

   Chorus

Skinamarink

A popular college song that's fun to horse around with.

Skin-a-ma-rink a-dink a-dink, Skin-a-ma-rink a-doo,

I love you;

Skin-a-ma-rink a-dink a-dink, Skin-a-ma-rink a-doo,

114

'Deed I do. I
love you in the mor-ning ___ and in the af-ter-noon; I
love you in the eve-ning ___ and un-der-neath the moon. Oh,

115

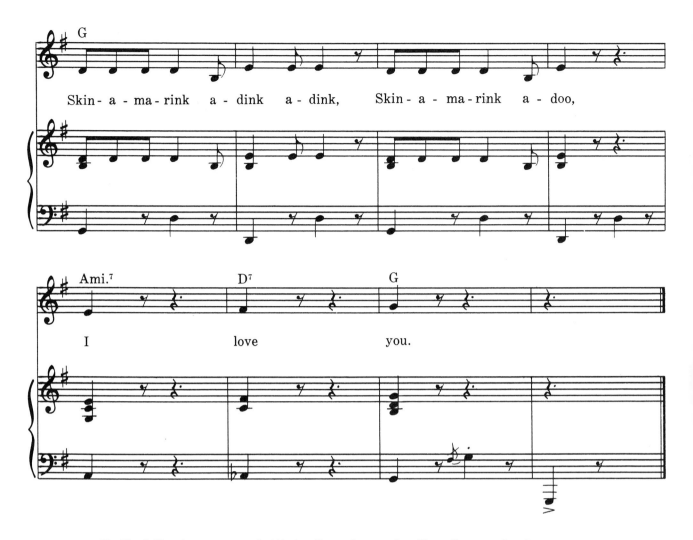

Skin- a - ma - rink a - dink a - dink, Skin- a - ma - rink a - doo,

I   love   you.

(In the following verses substitute other phrases for "love," squeezing in syllables by repeating the same note, if necessary.)

2. Skin-a-ma-rink a-dink a-dink,
   Skin-a-ma-rink a-doo,
   I madly-and-passionately-adore you;
   Skin-a-ma-rink a-dink a-dink,
   Skin-a-ma-rink a-doo,
   'Deed I do.

   I madly-and-passionately-adore you in the morning and in the afternoon;
   I madly-and-passionately-adore you in the evening and underneath the moon. Oh,
   Skin-a-ma-rink a-dink a-dink,
   Skin-a-ma-rink a-doo,
   I madly-and-passionately-adore you.

(Continue by substituting the following phrases in the appropriate places.)

3. I barely-tolerate you;

4. I run-as-fast-as-I-can-the-minute-I-see you;

5. I wish-I-understood you;

6. I wish-I-didn't-have-to-sit-next-to you;

   etc.

PART VI
HORSING AROUND

Parodies, puns, and sheer nonsense songs

The Captain's Shanty

The mystifying nautical terminology of the traditional sea shanties made sense to the sailing men who first sang them. Here is a parody by Elliot Crawford Finch with a catalogue of sea-shanty words that make no sense whatsoever. The last verse has only three lines, omitting the expected refrain "Yo-ho-ho and a ruddy-bum-bum"; but pause before singing the final chorus to trap those who forget and add the refrain line in its usual place.

Rousing

1. I've been a sai - lor since my birth,
2. Fif - teen years and we have-n't had a shore leave,

Yo - ho - ho and a rud - dy - bum - bum;

Took my home for all it's worth,
(spoken) Heave, heave, heave, heave,

118

Yo - ho - ho and a rud - dy - bum - bum.

Chorus:

Lime, scur - vy, am - ber - gris, and mar - ma - lade;

Hoist the pe - tard and we'll haul a - way, me bul - ly boys.

Lime, scur - vy, am - ber-gris, and blub-ber; We're

D   G

bound for Cin - cin - na - ti.

3. Sight the bowsprit, down the grog,
   Yo-ho-ho and a ruddy-bum-bum;
   Carve the turkey in the log,
   Yo-ho-ho and a ruddy-bum-bum.

   Chorus: Lime, scurvy, ambergris, and marmalade;
   Hoist the petard and we'll haul away, me bully boys.
   Lime, scurvy, ambergris, and blubber,
   We're bound for Cincinnati.

4. Come the day she's out of port,
   Yo-ho-ho and a ruddy-bum-bum;
   Keel the bosun or the thwart,
   Yo-ho-ho and a ruddy-bum-bum.

   Chorus

5. Through a fluke the spout did whale,
   Yo-ho-ho and a ruddy-bum-bum;
   But that's the end of my scrimshaw tale.
   (*Omit last refrain.*)

   Chorus

I Went to the Movies Tomorrow

An example of "tangle talk": a type of nonsense rhyme
made up of deliberate juxtapositions of incongruities.

Deadpan

1. I went to the mo-vies to-mor-row. _____ I
2. I said to the la-dy be-hind me, _____ "I

took a front seat at the back. _____ I fell from the floor to the
can-not see o-ver your hat." _____ I phoned for a tax-i and

bal-c'ny _____ And broke a front bone in my back.
walked it, _____ And that's why I nev-er came back.

Mixed-up Mother Goose

Anonymous parodies of familiar nursery songs

Scintillate

Simply

Scin - til - late, scin - til - late, glo - bule au - rif - ic!

Fain would I fath - om thy na - ture spe - cif - ic.

Loft - i - ly poised in the e - ther ca - pa - cious,

Strong-ly re - sem - bling a gem car - bon - a - ceous,

Scin - til - late, scin - til - late glo - bule au - rif - ic!

Fain I would fath - om thy na - ture spe - cif - ic.

123

London Bridge

Inanely

Lon - don Bridge is fal - ling up, fal - ling up, fal - ling up,

Lon - don Bridge is fal - ling up, my fair pick - le.

Mary Had a William Goat

Stupidly

1. Ma - ry had a Wil - liam goat, Wil - liam goat, Wil - liam goat,
Chorus: Whoop - dee - doo - den - doo - den - dah, doo - den - dah, doo - den - dah,

Ma - ry had a Wil - liam goat, and he was lined with zinc.
Whoop - dee - doo - den - doo - den - dah,___ doo - den - doo - den - dah.

Three Myopic Rodents

ex - cised their ex - tre - mi - ties with a car - ving u - ten - sil. Did you

ev - er re - gard such an oc - cur - rence in your ex - ist - ence As

three my - o - pic ro - dents?

My Bonnie

Gracefully

1. My Bon - nie looked in - to a gas tank,_____ The
2. My Bon - nie had a peach - bloom com - plex - ion;_____ Her

height of its con - tents to see._____ She
face it was love - ly to see._____ One

light - ed a match to as - sist her._____ Oh,
day she got caught in a rain - storm._____ Oh,

bring back my Bon - nie to me! _____
bring back her beau - ty to me! _____

Chorus:

Bring back, bring back, Oh, bring back my

Bon - nie to me, to me; Bring back,

bring back, Oh, bring back my Bon - nie to me! _____

After the Ball Was Over

This parody of the old popular song is probably better known now than the original.

Af - ter the ball was o - ver, She lay on the so - fa and sighed. _____ She put her false teeth in salt wa - ter And took out her love - ly glass eye. _____ She

130

kicked her cork leg in the cor - ner And hung up her

wig on the wall. _____ The rest of her went to

bye - byes, Af - ter the ball. _____

rit.

Springtime in the Rockies

A parody of the American popular song as it is sung by schoolchildren in Wales.

It was spring - time in the Rock - ies, _____ And the rain was

fal - ling fast. _____ A ____ bare - foot - ed tramp with

boots on ____ Came ___ slow - ly whiz - zing past. _____ He ____

went round a straight crook-ed cor-ner _____ To ___ see a dead

don - key die. _____ He ___ took out a pis-tol to

C   **Gmi.**

G⁷   **C⁷**   **F**

stab him, _____ And ___ shot him-self right in the eye. _____

The Song of the Salvation Army

A parody of the pious, and often unintentionally comical, temperance songs of the early part of this century.

With accented fervor

1. We're com-ing, we're com-ing, our brave lit-tle band. On the right side of tem-p'rance we now take our stand. We don't use to-bac-co, be-cause we all think That the peo-ple who use it are like-ly to drink!

2. We ne-ver eat cook-ies, be-cause they have yeast And one lit-tle bite makes a man like a beast. Oh, can you im-ag-ine a sad-der dis-grace Than a man in the gut-ter with crumbs on his face?

Chorus:

A - way, a - way with rum, by gum, with rum, by gum, with rum,___ by gum! A - way, a - way with rum, by gum, The song of the Sal - va - tion Ar - my.

3. We never eat fruitcake, because it has rum
   And one little slice puts a man on the bum.
   Oh, can you imagine a sorrier sight
   Than a man eating fruitcake until he gets tight?

Chorus: Away, away with rum, by gum,
   With rum, by gum, with rum, by gum!
   Away, away with rum, by gum,
   The song of the Salvation Army.

A Stately Song

One of the many punning songs on State names—this one omitting the most obvious verse about Della Wearing her New Jersey.

Lightly martial

1. If Ma - ry goes far out to sea, By way - ward breez - es fanned,— I'd
2. If Ten - ny went high up in air And looked o'er land and lea,— Looked

like to know, can you tell me, Just where would Ma - ry - land? Oh,
here and there and ev - 'ry-where, Pray, what would Ten - nes - see? Oh,

3. I looked out of the window and
Saw Orry on the lawn.
He's not there now, and who can tell
Just where has Oregon?
Oh, where has Oregon, oh, where has Oregon?
He's not there now, and who can tell
Just where has Oregon?

where would Ma - ry - land, _____ oh, where would Ma - ry - land? _____ I'd
what would Ten - nes - see, _____ oh, what would Ten - nes - see? _____ Looked

like to know, can you tell me, Just where would Ma - ry - land?
here and there and ev - 'ry - where, Pray, what would Ten - nes - see?

4. Two girls were quarreling one day
   With gardening tools, and so
   I said, "My dears, let Mary rake,
   And just let Idaho.
   Oh, just let Idaho, oh, just let Idaho";
   I said, "My dears, let Mary rake,
   And just let Idaho!"

Midnight on the Ocean

Another, less familiar "tangle talk" song.

1. 'Twas mid - night on the o - cean; _____ Not a street - car was in sight. _____ The sun was shin - ing bright - ly; It was rain - ing all the night.

2. 'Twas a sum - mer's day in win - ter, _____ And the rain was snow - ing fast _____ As the bare - foot girl with shoes on Stood there sit - ting on the grass.

3. 'Twas evening, and the sunrise
Was just setting in the west,
And the fishes in the treetops
Were all cuddled in their nests.

4. As the wind was blowing bubbles,
Lightning flashed from left to right;
Everything that you could see
Was hidden out of sight.

5. The boats sailed up the highway,
For the bridges were all down,
And the dogs barked from the rooftops
In that sad and silent town.

6. 'Twas midnight on the ocean;
Not a streetcar was in sight.
The sun was shining brightly;
It was raining all the night.

My Nose Is Blue

A musical setting of a favorite poem from Alexander Soames, *by Karla Kuskin.*

Truly True

One of the Songs of the Pogo, *with words by Walt Kelly and music by Norman Monath.*

Lazily gamboling

Gam - bo - ling on the gum - bo _____ with the gam - bits all in gear, _____ I daffed up - on a dil - ly _____ who would be my dol - ly dear. _____

Oh, Dil - ly, I would dal - ly _____ if you'd be but

tru - ly true. _____ How sil - ly! I must

sal - ly off to do my du - ly do. _____

Rules

A musical setting of a favorite poem from Alexander Soames, *by Karla Kuskin.*
This song must gain momentum as it goes along and end with an explosion at the final "do not!"

Do not smoke ci - gars on so - fas. Do not dance on vel - vet chairs.

Do not take a whale to vis - it Rus - sell's moth - er's cous - in's yacht.

And what - ev - er else you do do, It is bet - ter you do not!

Three Craw

The fun of this nonsense song is to sing it in an exaggerated Scottish accent, rolling all the r's and pronouncing the words briskly.

1. The three craw sat up-on a wa', sat up-on a wa', sat up-on a wa' - a' - a' - a'; The three craw sat up-on a wa' on a cold and frost-y mor - nin'.

2. The first craw could-na' find his ma, could-na' find his ma, could-na' find his ma' a - a - a; The first craw could-na' find his ma on a cold and frost-y mor - nin'.

3. The second craw couldna' find his pa, couldna' find his pa, couldna' find his pa-a-a-a; The second craw couldna' find his pa on a cold and frosty mornin'.

4. The third craw couldna' fly at a', couldna' fly at a', couldna' fly at a'-a'-a'-a; The third craw couldna' fly at a' on a cold and frosty mornin'.

5. The fourth craw wasna' there at a', wasna' there at a', wasna' there at a'-a'-a'-a'; The fourth craw wasna' there at a' on a cold and frosty mornin'.

The Old Family Toothbrush

A parody of a sentimental old favorite, "The Old Oaken Bucket."

Nostalgically

1. The old fam-'ly tooth-brush, That dir-ty old tooth-brush, That sli-my old tooth-brush That hangs by the door.

2. First it was Fa-ther's, ___ Then it was Moth-er's, ___ Next it was Sis-ter's And now it is mine.

3. Oh Father he used it,
Mother abused it,
Sister refused it,
And now it is mine.

4. The old fam'ly toothbrush,
That dirty old toothbrush,
That slimy old toothbrush
That hangs by the door.

145

PART VII
FUNNY, TALL, AND TRAGICAL TALES

Bluebeard

The old story with a new ending.

Trippingly

C   G⁷

1. A mai - den from the Bos - po - rus with eyes as bright as phos - pho - rus Once
2. It might be men-tioned ca - sual - ly that blue as lap - is la - zu - li He

C   Ami.   Dmi.   G⁷

wed the might - y bai - liff of the ca - liph of Ke - lat. Though
dyed his lips, his la - shes, his mus - ta - ches, and his beard. And

C   G⁷

di - li - gent and zea - lous, he was some - what prone to jea - lous - y. (Con-
just be - cause he did it, he a - roused his wife's ti - mid - i - ty. Her

C   Ami.   Dmi.   G⁷   C

sid - er - ing her beau - ty, 'twas his du - ty to be that!)
ter - ror she dis - sem - bled, yet she trem - bled when he neared.

Chorus — Faster and more boisterous:

Yu- az - ur- am, oh, yu- az- ur- am, __ Glo- ry hal-le- lu- jah, yu- az - ur- am.

3. This feeling insalubrious soon made her most lugubrious,
   And bitterly she missed her elder sister, Mary Ann.
   She asked if she might write her to come down and spend a night or two,
   And Bluebeard answered rightly and politely, "Yes, you can!"

   Chorus: Yu-az-ur-am, oh, yu-az-ur-am,
   Glory hallelujah, yu-az-ur-am.

Chorus   4. When business would necessitate a journey, he would hesitate,
   But fearing to mistrust her, he would trust her with the keys,
   Bidding her most prayerfully, "I beg you use them carefully.
   Don't look what I deposit in the closet, if you please."

Chorus   5. Bluebeard, the Monday following, his jealous feeling swallowing,
   Packed all his clothes together in a leather-bound valise.
   And, feigning reprehensibly, he started out, ostensibly,
   By traveling to learn a bit of Smyrna and of Greece.

Chorus   6. His wife made but a cursory inspection of the nursery.
   The kitchen and the airy little dairy were a bore;
   Likewise the large and scanty rooms, the billiard, bath, and anterooms;
   But not that interdicted and restricted little door!

Chorus   7. At last, her curiosity awakened by the closet he
   So carefully had hidden and forbidden her to see,
   This damsel disobedient did something inexpedient,
   And in the keyhole tiny turned the shiny little key!

Chorus   8. She shrieked aloud convulsively and started back repulsively:
   Ten heads of girls he'd wedded and beheaded met her eye!
   And turning round, most terrified, her darkest fears were verified,
   For Bluebeard stood behind her, come to find her on the sly!

Chorus   9. Perceiving she was fated to be seen decapitated too,
   She telegraphed her brothers and some others what she feared;
   And Sister Anne looked out for them, in readiness to shout for them
   Whenever in the distance with assistance they appeared.

Chorus   10. But only, from the battlement, she saw some dust that cattle meant.
   The ordinary story isn't gory, it's a jest!
   For here's the truth unqualified: her husband *wasn't* mollified.
   Her head is in his bloody little study with the rest!

Shootin' with Rasputin

The verses should be sung slowly and schmaltzily, à la Gypsy, while the last six lines of the chorus ought to proceed as quickly and boisterously as clarity permits.

Very freely, with great sentiment

Dmi.   Gmi.

1. An in - ti - mate friend of the Czar was I, A
2. A friend of the Czar was I all his life, But

Dmi.   A⁷

per - son - al friend of the great Ni - ko - lai. We
friend - li - er still was ___ I with his wife. We

D   Gmi.

prac - tic - 'ly slept in the same dou - ble bed; It was
prac - tic - 'ly slept in the same dou - ble bed, Till the

3. But one awful day, revolution broke out.
   I failed to see what the fuss was about,
   But after a while I bade Russia goodbye:
   It was simply a case of Lenin or I.

   Chorus: But all that seems distant, and all that seems far
   From those glorious days at the palace of the Czar
   When I went shootin' with Rasputin,
   Ate farina with Czarina,
   Blintzes with the princes and the Czar, hey, hey, hey!
   We were sharin' tea and herring,
   Dipped banana in smetana,
   Borscht and wurst around the samovar.

The ship Titanic

Though the chorus proclaims "It was sad," this remains one of the jolliest descriptions of disaster ever. Innumerable children who first heard the name Titanic in group singing around a campfire are appalled in later years to learn that 1,513 lives were lost on April 15, 1912, "when that great ship went down."

Dynamically

1. Oh, they built the ship Ti - tan - ic to sail the o - cean blue, And they
2. Oh, they sailed ___ from ___ Eng - land, and al - most reached the shore When the

thought they had a ship that the wa - ter would nev - er go through. It was
rich re - fused to as - so - ci - ate with ___ the poor, So they

on her maid - en trip that an ice - berg hit the ship. It was
put them down be - low, where they were the first to go. It was

sad ___ when that great ___ ship went down.
sad ___ when that great ___ ship went down.

Chorus:

Oh, it was sad ___ (It was sad), It was sad ___ (It was sad), It was

sad when that great ___ ship went down (to the bot - tom of the)

Hus - bands and wives, lit - tle bit - ty chil - dren lost their lives. It was

sad ___ when that great ___ ship went down.

3. Oh, the boat was full of sin and the sides about to burst
   When the captain shouted, "A-women and children first!"
   Oh, the captain tried to wire, but the lines were all on fire.
   It was sad when that great ship went down.

   Chorus: Oh, it was sad (It was sad),
       It was sad (It was sad),
       Husbands and wives, little bitty children lost their lives.
       It was sad when that great ship went down.

4. Oh, they swung the lifeboats out o'er the deep and raging sea
   When the band struck up with "Nearer My God to Thee."
   Little children wept and cried as the waves swept o'er the side.
   It was sad when that great ship went down.

   Chorus

Bible Stories

Surely one of the longest Bible songs ever written, and probably the most irreverent as well.

Instructively

F   C⁷

1. Young folks, old folks, ev - 'ry-bod - y come,
2. Ad - am was a gar - den - er, and Eve she was his spouse. They

F

Come and join our Sun - day School; Make your-self at home.
got the sack for stea - ling food and went to keep - ing house. They

B♭   Gmi.

Please to check your chew - ing gum and ra - zors at the door, And you'll
lived a ve - ry qui - et life, and peace - ful in the main, Un -

hear some Bi - ble sto - ries that you've nev - er heard be - fore.
til they had a ba - by and star - ted rais - ing Cain.

3. Noah was a mariner who sailed around the sea,
   With a half a dozen wives and a big menagerie.
   He failed the first season when it rained for forty days,
   For in that sort of weather, no circus ever pays.

4. Esau was a cowboy of the wild and woolly make.
   Half the farm belonged to him, and half belonged to Jake.
   Now, Esau thought his title to the farm was none too clear,
   So he sold it out to Jakey for a sandwich and a beer.

5. Joseph was a shepherd, too; he kept his father's goats.
   His father used to dress him in the very loudest coats.
   His brothers they got jealous, and they threw him in a well.
   Joseph went to heaven and the others went to—

6. Pharaoh had a daughter; she had a winsome smile.
   She found the infant Moses afloating on the Nile.
   She took him to her father with the old familiar tale,
   Which is just about as probable as Jonah and the whale.

7. Jonah was an emigrant, so runs the Bible tale;
   He took a steerage passage in a transatlantic whale.
   Jonah in the belly of the whale felt quite compressed,
   So he pushed a little button, and the whale did all the rest.

8. Samson was a husky guy, as everyone should know,
   He used to lift five hundred pounds as strongman for the show.
   One week the bill was rotten and the actors had a souse,
   But the strongman act of Samson's it just brought down the house.

9. David was a shepherd boy, a plucky little cuss.
   Along came Goliath alooking for a fuss.
   David took a slingshot and socked him on the crust;
   Goliath reeled a couple times, and then he bit the dust.

10. Ahab had a lively wife whose name was Jezebel.
    She went out in the vineyard to hang the clothes, and fell.
    "She's gone to the dogs," the people told the king;
    Ahab said he'd never heard of such a doggone thing!

11. God made Satan, and Satan made sin.
    God made a hot place to put Satan in.
    Satan didn't like it, so he said he wouldn't stay.
    He's been acting like the devil ever since that sorry day.

12. Salome was a dancer, and she danced before the king.
    She wiggled and she wobbled, and she shook most everything.
    The king said to Salome, "We'll have no scandal here."
    "I wouldn't be so sure," she said, and kicked the chandelier.

Dunderbeck

*A song reminiscent of Upton Sinclair's famous exposé of dark doings in the
Chicago stockyards, The Jungle: the ingredients that make up the sausages seem to be the same.*

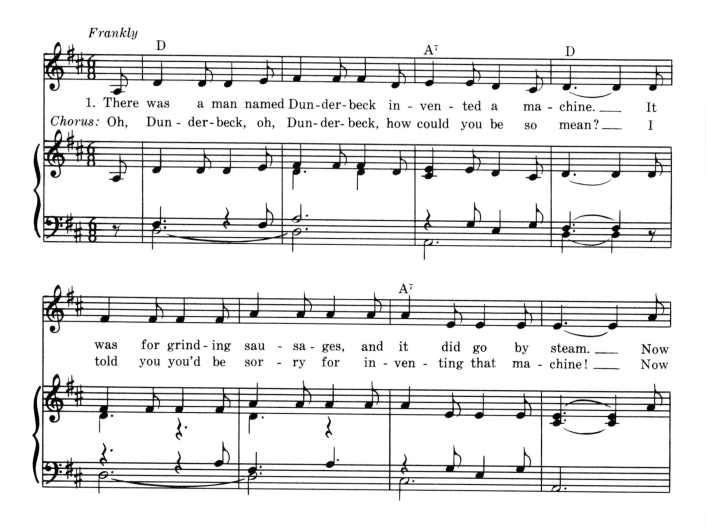

Frankly

1. There was a man named Dun-der-beck in-ven-ted a ma-chine. ___ It
Chorus: Oh, Dun-der-beck, oh, Dun-der-beck, how could you be so mean? ___ I

was for grind-ing sau-sa-ges, and it did go by steam. ___ Now
told you you'd be sor-ry for in-ven-ting that ma-chine! ___ Now

2. Now, one fine day a little boy came in the butcher store.
   There was a pound of sausage meat alying on the floor,
   And while the boy was waiting, he began to hum a tune.
   The sausage meat began to jump and skip around the room.

   Chorus: Oh, Dunderbeck, oh, Dunderbeck, how could you be so mean?
   I told you you'd be sorry for inventing that machine!
   Now all the neighbors' cats and dogs will nevermore be seen;
   They'll all be ground in sausages in Dunderbeck's machine.

all the neigh-bors' cats and dogs will nev-er-more be seen; They'll _
all the neigh-bors' cats and dogs will nev-er-more be seen; They'll _

all be ground in sau - sa - ges in Dun - der - beck's ma - chine.
all be ground in sau - sa - ges in Dun - der - beck's ma - chine.

3. Now, something was the matter: that machine it wouldn't go.
So Dunderbeck crawled right inside to see what's wrong, you know.
His wife she had a nightmare and was walking in her sleep;
She grabbed the crank and gave a yank, and Dunderbeck was meat!

Chorus

The Mermaid

A possibly unintentional musical joke is concealed in this jolly song of disaster at sea when the tune descends for the words "skipping to the top" and rises triumphantly for the landlubbers who "lie down below, below, below, below."

Rolling along

1. 'Twas Fri - day___ morn when we ___ set ___ sail, And we
2. Then up spake the cap - tain of our ___ gal - lant ship, And a

were not far from the land When the cap - tain ___ spied a
fine old cap - tain was he: "This ___ fish - y ___ mer - maid has

mer - maid so fair, With a comb and a brush in her hand.
warned me of our doom; We shall sink to the bot - tom of the sea."

Chorus:

Oh, the o - cean waves may roll (Let 'em roll), And the storm - y winds may

blow (Let 'em blow), But we poor ___ sail - ors go

skip - ping to the top, While the land - lub - bers lie down be -

low, be - low, be - low, While the land - lub - bers lie down be - low.

3. Then up spake the cook of our gallant ship,
   And a crazy old cook was he:
   "I care much more for my kettles and my pans
   Than I do for the bottom of the sea."

   Chorus: Oh, the ocean waves may roll (Let 'em roll),
   And the stormy winds may blow (Let 'em blow),
   But we poor sailors go skipping to the top,
   While the landlubbers lie down below, below, below,
   While the landlubbers lie down below.

4. Then up spake the cabin boy of our gallant ship,
   And a dirty little rat was he:
   "There's nary a soul in old Salem town
   Who gives a darn about me."

   Chorus

5. (Slowly)
   Then three times round went our gallant ship,
   And three times round went she;
   Then three times round went our gallant ship,
   And she sank to the bottom of the sea.

   Chorus

Clementine

An old American folk song that became popular on college campuses, where some of the later verses must have originated.

Zesty

1. In a cav-ern, in a can-yon, ex-ca-va-ting for a mine, Dwelt a
2. Light she was and like a fai-ry, and her shoes were num-ber nine; Her-ring

mi-ner, for-ty-ni-ner, and his daugh-ter Clem-en-tine.
box-es with-out top-ses san-dals were for Clem-en-tine.

3. Drove she ducklings to the water every morning just at nine.
   Hit her foot against a splinter, fell into the foaming brine.

   Chorus: Oh, my darling, oh, my darling, oh, my darling Clementine,
   You are lost and gone forever! Dreadful sorry, Clementine.

4. Ruby lips above the water blowing bubbles soft and fine;
   But alas, I was no swimmer, so I lost my Clementine.

   Chorus

Chorus:

Oh, my dar - ling, oh, my dar - ling, oh, my dar - ling Clem-en-tine, You are lost and gone for-ev - er! Dread-ful sor - ry, Clem-en - tine.

5. Listen Boy Scouts, heed the warning of this tragic tale of mine:
   Artificial respiration could have saved my Clementine.

   Chorus

6. How I missed her, how I missed her, how I missed my Clementine!
   Then I kissed her little sister and forgot my Clementine.

   Chorus

Nothing Else to Do

May Irwin, one of the great comediennes of the 1890's, was sometimes called "the stage mother of ragtime." This was one of her most popular hits.

Steady and jazzy

1. A - way down yon-der in the Yank-e - ty Yank, A bull-frog jumped from
2. When they bur-ied that frog,___ the preach - er said, "The rea - son why this young

bank to bank 'Cause there was-n't noth-in' else to do. ___ He
frog is dead: 'Cause there was-n't noth-in' else to do. ___ And

stubbed his toe and in he fell, And the neigh-bors all say that he
all you frogs just a- listen to me: You___ bet - ter stay home with your

went to — well, 'Cause he had - n't noth - in' else to do. ___
fam - i - ly, When you have - n't noth - in' else to do." ___

Chorus—faster and rollicking:

And just lots of folks are like that foo-lish frog o' mine,___ A-run-

ning in - to trou - ble just to pass the time, And ____ And the

dev - il's al - ways loaf - ing round here just to grab the kind That

nev - er has - n't noth - ing else to do.____

165

The Fatal Curse of Drink

A parody of the moralistic temperance songs of the last century, this song must be sung as seriously and sentimentally as possible.

Quasi-recitative

1. There was a poor young man, and he came ___ to New York To
2. One night when he went out with his new-found friends to dine, They

find him-self a lu -cra-tive po -si -tion be- fit - ting his tal - ents. Now, he
tried to per-suade him to take a drink. ___ They

haun -ted all the em -ploy -ment a -gen - cies, But he was
temp -ted him and temp -ted him, but he re -

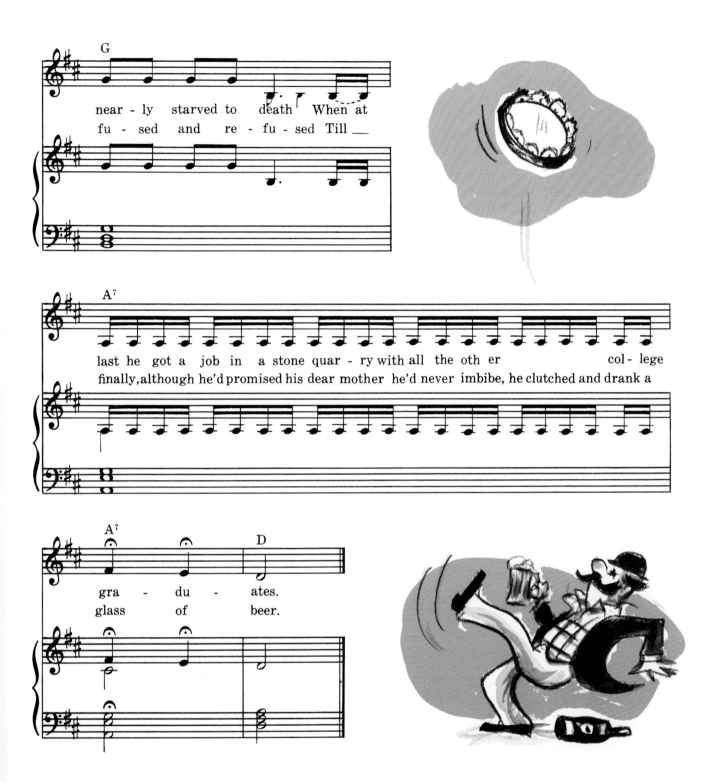

near - ly starved to death When at
fu - sed and re - fu - sed Till___

last he got a job in a stone quar - ry with all the oth er col - lege
finally, although he'd promised his dear mother he'd never imbibe, he clutched and drank a

gra - du - ates.
glass of beer.

3. When he seen what he had did, he dashed the liquor to the floor
   And staggered out the door with delirium tremens.
   While in the throes of liquor he met a Salvation Army lassie,
   And cruelly (with one sharp but well-aimed kick) he broke her tambourine.

4. When she seen what he had did, she placed a mark upon his brow
   With a kick that she had learned from before she was saved.
   So kind friends, take my advice and shun the fatal curse of drink,
   And don't go around breaking people's tambourines.

The Crocodile

A tall story from Nova Scotia.

Verse 1: One day when I was sailing The country to explore, storm came up and wrecked the ship And drove me to the shore,

Verse 2: Just then it was I sighted A fearsome crocodile. From the tip of his nose to the end of his tail He was ten thousand mile,

Chorus: With me right va-la-ri-ty, whack va-la-ri-ty, Chock va-la-ri-ty day.

3. That crocodile was clearly
   A diff'rent sort of race;
   I had to climb a mighty pine
   To look into his face,

   Chorus: With me right valarity,
   whack valarity,
   Chock valarity day.

4. I started to sail off then,
   With ev'ry stitch of sail,
   And going nine knots by the log,
   In ten months reached his tail,

   Chorus

5. The crocodile he yawned,
   And he thought he had his victim,
   But I went down his throat, you see,
   And that is how I tricked him,

   Chorus

PART VIII
GRUESOME, GRISLY, AND MEAN

Blood on the Saddle

No one knows if this old cowboy song was ever taken seriously. (Probably not.)

Stoically

1. There was blood on __ the sad-dle and blood on the ground, And a
2. Oh, the cow-boy __ lay in it, all cov - ered with gore, And he

great big pud-dle __ of blood all a - round.
won't go a - ri - ding __ his bron - co no more.

3. Oh, pity the cowboy, all bloody and red;
His bronco fell on him and mashed in his head.

170

The Scary Song

This song should be sung as evenly and monotonously as possible to make the final shriek at the end most effective. Once a group has sung this song, a new and unsuspecting victim is needed before the group can sing it again.

Note: Each verse is followed by a single octave in the left hand one-half step lower until the song is over.

3. One night she thought she'd take a walk,
   Oo-oo-oo-oo.

4. She walked down by the old graveyard,
   Oo-oo-oo-oo.

5. She saw the bones all lying about,
   Oo-oo-oo-oo.

6. She went to the corner to get a broom,
   Oo-oo-oo-oo.

7. She opened the door, and
   EEEEEK! (*Everybody shrieks wildly.*)

They're Moving Grandpa's Grave

An old British music-hall song.

Indignantly

1. They're mov-ing grand-pa's grave to build a sew-er; ____ They're
what's the use of hav-ing a re-li-gion, ____ And

mov-ing it re-gard-less of ex-pense. They're
think-ing when you're dead your trou-bles cease, If

Dmi.

Verses 1, 2, 3

shift-ing his re-mains to put in nine-inch drains, To
some rich ci-ty crank wants a pipe-line to his tank And they'll

ir - ri - gate some plush bloke's res - i - dence.   2. Now,

nev - er let a work - man sleep in peace.

Verse 4

4. have their blee-ding nerve To muck a - bout a Brit-ish work-man's grave. _____

rit.

3. Now, Grandpa in his life was not a quitter,
And I don't suppose he'll be a quitter now,
'Cause when the job's complete, he'll haunt the privy seat,
And he'll only let them go when he'll allow.

4. And won't there be some bleeding consternation,
And won't them city toffs begin to rave,
But they'll get what they deserve, for they had the bleeding
    nerve
To muck about a British workman's grave.

In the Boardinghouse

To the tune of "Silver Threads Among the Gold."

Lovingly

1. In the board-ing house where I live,
2. When the dog died, we had hot dogs;

Ev - 'ry-thing is grow-ing old.
When the cat died, cat - nip tea.

Sil - ver threads are in the but - ter;
When the land - lord died, I left there:

All the bread has turned to mold.
Spare - ribs were too much for me.

MacTavish

A grisly song to the tune of "The Irish Washerwoman."

Gleefully

Oh, Mac - Tav - ish is dead and his broth - er don't know it. His

broth - er is dead and Mac - Tav - ish don't know it. They're

both of them dead and they're in the same bed,____ And

nei - ther one knows that the oth - er is dead.

Don't Swat Your Mother

A burlesque of the sentimental "mother" songs of the last century.

Wickedly, beerily

D G D

Don't swat your moth- er, boys, just 'cause she's old!   Don't mop the

A⁷

floor with her face.＿＿＿   Think how her love is a

The Worm Song

An impossibly cheerful tune keeps this from being the most gruesome song ever written.

Ghostlike Emi.

1. Did you ev - er think, as the hearse rolls by, That
men with shov - els will __ stand a - round; They'll

soon - er or la - ter you're go - ing to die, And the
shov - el you in - to that cold, __ wet ground. 2. Oh, the 3. through with you!

End of last verse B⁷ Emi.

B⁷

2. Oh, the worms crawl in and the worms crawl out;
   The worms crawl everywhere round about.
   Then each one takes just a bite or two
   Of something or other that used to be you.

3. Oh, your eyes drop out and your teeth fall in,
   And the worms crawl over your mouth and your chin.
   They bring all their friends and their friends' friends too,
   And there's nothing much left when they're through with you!

Nell Flaherty's Drake

A deliciously mean Irish street ballad with one of the most comprehensive catalogs of invective in all of folk literature.

Vengefully

C   Ami.

1. My name it is Nell, and quite can - did I tell, That I
2. May his pig nev - er grunt; may his cat nev - er hunt; That a

C   G⁷

live near Coote Hill I will nev - er de - ny. I
ghost may him haunt in the dead of the night. May his

had a large drake, the___ truth for to spake, That my

hen nev - er lay; may his ass nev - er bray; May his

grand - moth - er left me, and she goin' to die. He was

goat fly a - way like an old pa - per kite. That the

whole - some and sound and he weighed twen - ty pound, And the

flies and the fleas may the wretch ev - er tease, And a

3. May his pipe never smoke and his teapot be broke;
And to add to the joke, may his kettle ne'er boil.
May he ne'er rest in bed till the hour he is dead;
May he always be fed upon fish-liver oil.
May he swell with the gout till his grinders fall out;
May he roar, bawl, and shout with a horrid toothache;
May his temples wear horns and all his toes corns,
The monster that murdered Nell Flaherty's drake.

C   **F**   **D⁷**   **G⁷**

u - ni - verse round I would rove for his sake. Bad
bit - ter north breeze make him trem - ble and shake; May a

C   **Ami.**

wind to the rob - ber, both drunk - en and so - ber, That
four - year - old bug make a nest in the lug Of the

C   **F**   **G⁷**   **C**

mur - dered Nell Fla - her - ty's beau - ti - ful drake.
mon - ster that mur - dered Nell Fla - her - ty's drake.

4. May his spade never dig; may his sow never pig;
May each nit in his wig be as large as a snail.
May his door have no latch; may his house have no thatch;
May his turkey not hatch; may the rats eat his kale.
May ev'ry old fairy from Cork to Dunleary
Dip him snug and airy in some pond or lake,
Where the eel and the trout may dine on the snout
Of the monster that murdered Nell Flaherty's drake.

Nothing Whatever to Grumble at

Words by W. S. Gilbert, music by Arthur Sullivan, from the operetta Princess Ida.

Brightly

The piano introduction and interludes can of course be omitted.

Dmi.

1. When - e'er I poke sar - cas - tic joke, re -
2. I've of - fered gold in sums un - told to

plete with mal - ice spite - ful, The peo - ple vile po - lite - ly smile and
all who'd con - tra - dict me. I've said I'd pay a pound a day to

vote me quite de - light - ful!   Now, when a wight sits
an - y - one - who kicked me!   I've bribed with toys great

up all night ill - na - tured jokes de - vi - sing And all his wiles are
vul - gar boys to ut - ter some - thing spite - ful, But bless you, no, they

183

met with smiles, it's hard, there's no dis - gui - sing! Ah! _____ Oh,
will be so con - foun - ded - ly po - lite - ful! Ah! _____ In

don't the days seem lank and long when all goes right and no-thing goes wrong, And
short, these ag - gra - va - ting lads, they tick-le my tastes, they feed _ my fads, They

isn't your life ex - treme - ly flat with no-thing what-ev-er to grum - ble at?
give me this and they give me that, and I've no-thing what-ev-er to grum - ble at!

On to the Morgue

A travesty based on Chopin's funeral march, collected by Carl Sandburg at a labor-union convention.

Inexorably

1. On to the morgue; that's the on-ly place for me. On to the morgue; that's the on-ly place for me. Take it from the head one, He is sure a dead one.

2. Where will we all be one hun-dred years from now? Where will we all be one hun-dred years from now? Push-ing up the dai-sies, push-ing up the dai-sies:

On to the morgue, that's the on-ly place for me.
That's where we'll all be one hun-dred years from now.

Rickety Tickety Tin

The Irish Ballad

A pseudo—folk song by Tom Lehrer about a mass murderess with an interesting sense of values.

1. A - bout a mai - den I'll sing a song, Sing rick - et - y tick - et - y tin, ____ A - bout a mai - den I'll sing a song, Who did - n't have ___ her fam - 'ly long. Not on - ly did ___ she do them wrong: She ___

2. One mor - ning, in ___ a fit of pique, Sing rick - et - y tick - et - y tin, ____ One morn - ing, in ___ a fit of pique, She drowned her fa - ther in the creek. The wa - ter tas - ted bad for a week, And we ___

did ev-'ry one of them in, _____ them in, _____ She
had to make do _____ with gin, _____ with gin, _____ We

did ev-'ry one of them in. _____
had to make do _____ with gin. _____

3. Her mother she could never stand,
   Sing rickety tickety tin;
   Her mother she could never stand,
   And so a cyanide soup she planned.
   The mother died with the spoon in her hand,
   Her face in a hideous grin, a grin,
   Her face in a hideous grin.

4. She set her sister's hair on fire,
   Sing rickety tickety tin;
   She set her sister's hair on fire,
   And as the smoke and flames rose higher,
   She danced around the funeral pyre,
   Playing a violin, -olin,
   Playing a violin.

5. She weighted her brother down with stones,
   Sing rickety tickety tin;
   She weighted her brother down with stones
   And sent him off to Davy Jones,
   And all they ever found were some bones
   And occasional pieces of skin, of skin,
   And occasional pieces of skin.

6. One day when she had nothing to do,
   Sing rickety tickety tin,
   One day when she had nothing to do,
   She cut her baby brother in two
   And served him up as an Irish stew
   And invited the neighbors in, -bors in,
   And invited the neighbors in.

7. And when at last the police came by,
   Sing rickety tickety tin,
   And when at last the police came by,
   Her little pranks she did not deny;
   To do so she would have had to lie,
   And lying, she knew, was a sin, a sin,
   And lying, she knew, was a sin.

8. My tragic tale I won't prolong,
   Sing rickety tickety tin;
   My tragic tale I won't prolong,
   And if you do not enjoy my song,
   You've yourself to blame if it's too long:
   You should never have let me begin, begin,
   You should never have let me begin.

A Horrible Tale

A student song of the last century that is a remarkable precursor of the "sick" songs and stories of recent years.

Sarcastically

1. A hor-ri-ble tale I have to tell Of sad dis-as-ters
2. One day__ this dole-ful, dis-mal lot So dread-ful mel-an-

that be-fell A__ fam-i-ly that once re-si-ded
cho-ly got That an end to them-selves they did a-gree, Just as

Just in the ve-ry same__ thor-ough-fare as I did.
soon as they set-tled on which end__ it would be.__

For, oh, it is such a hor-ri-ble tale, 'Twill make your fa - ces

all turn pale; Your eyes with grief will be o - ver - come.

Twee - dle — twad - dle — twid -dle twad-dle twum!

3. First the father took a walk
   And cut his throat with a lump of chalk.
   Then the mother an end to herself she put
   By hanging herself in the water butt.

   Chorus: **(sarcastically)**

   > For, oh, it is such a horrible tale,
   > 'Twill make your faces all turn pale;
   > Your eyes with grief will be overcome.
   > Tweedle, twaddle, twiddle, twaddle, twum!

4. Then the sister went down on her knees
   And smothered herself in toasted cheese.
   But the brother was such a determined young fellow,
   He went and he poisoned himself with his umbrella.

   Chorus

5. Then the baby in the cradle
   Shot itself dead with the silver ladle.
   When the servant girl saw what he did,
   She strangled herself with a saucepan lid.

   Chorus

6. So here's a moral, if you choose:
   Don't ever give way to the blues,
   Or you may come to the dreadful ends
   Of these, my dismal, melancholy friends.

   Chorus

Nobody Likes Me

A perfect (although unappetizing) antidote for self-pity
with a cheerful, catchy tune to belie the morbid message.

With bravado

1. No - bo - dy likes me; ev - 'ry - bo - dy hates me.
2. The long, thin, sli - my ones slip down eas - i - ly; The

Go - ing to the gar - den to eat worms: Long, thin, sli - my ones,
short, fat, fuz - zy ones stick. When the short, fat, fuz - zy ones

short, fat, fuz - zy ones. Oo - ey, goo - ey, goo - ey, goo - ey worms
stick to ___ your teeth, Your blood _____ goes _____ ick!

3. So you bite off the heads, and spit out the tails,
   And throw the skins away;
   And nobody knows how I can survive
   On a hundred worms a day.

190

PART IX
FUNNY ROUNDS AND EASY HARMONIES

Little Tommy Tinker

In this four-part round, as the members of each group sing the word "Ma!"
they all rise and throw their hands up, sit down, and then bounce up with the
same motion for the second "Ma!"

Energetically

1. Lit - tle Tom - my Tink - er was burned by a clink - er, And

2. he be - gan to cry:

3. Ma! _____ Ma! _____

4. Poor lit - tle in - no - cent boy.

A Boat, a Boat

Merrily

1. A boat, a boat to cross the fer - ry

2. And we'll go o - ver and be mer - ry,

3. And as _____ we _____ float, sing, "Hey down der - ry."

192

Let Simon's Beard Alone

Politely

Let Si - mon's beard a - lone, a - lone, Let

'Tis no dis - grace to Si - mon's face, For

Then mock not, nor scoff not, nor jeer not, nor sneer not, But

Si - mon's beard a - lone.

he had nev - er one.

rath - er him be - moan.

Sandy McNab

Reproachfully

1.
There was an old fel - low named San - dy Mc - Nab

2.
Who had for his sup - per a ve - ry fine crab

3.
And had to be car - ried home in a cab.

'Tis Women Makes Us Love

Sadly, mournfully

1. 'Tis wom - en makes us love, _____

2. 'Tis love that makes us sad, _____

3. 'Tis sad - ness makes us drink, _____

4. And drink - ing makes us mad. _____

Banbury Ale

Boisterously

1. Ban - bur - y ale!

2. Where, where, where?

3. At the black - smith's house, I

4. would I were there.

Roll the R

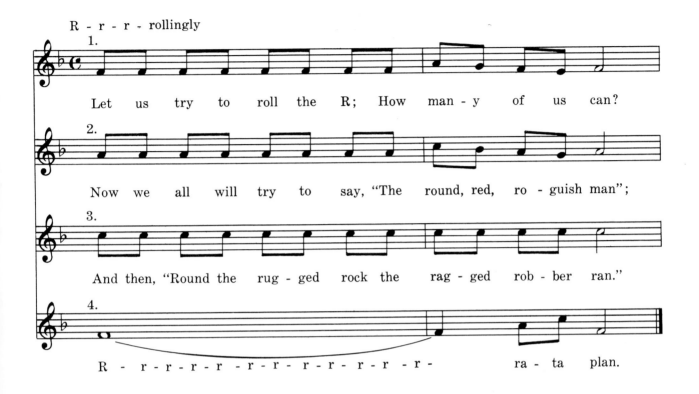

R - r - r - rollingly

1.
Let us try to roll the R; How man-y of us can?

2.
Now we all will try to say, "The round, red, ro - guish man";

3.
And then, "Round the rug - ged rock the rag - ged rob - ber ran."

4.
R - r - r - r - r - r - r - r - r - r - r - r - r -   ra - ta   plan.

Now We'll Make the Rafters Ring

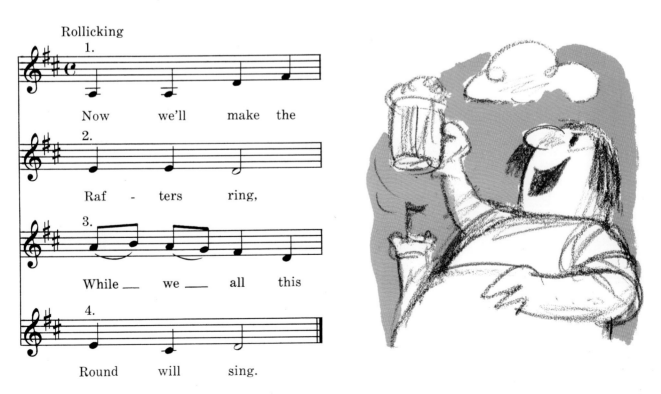

Rollicking

1.
Now   we'll   make   the

2.
Raf - ters   ring,

3.
While ___ we ___ all   this

4.
Round   will   sing.

Zum Gali Gali

First the whole group sings the chant through twice. Then, as half the group continues singing the chant, the other half sings the solo twice. The groups may then switch parts, with the chanters taking on the solo and the solo singers taking over the chant.

The simple Hebrew words of this Israeli folk song mean "The pioneer is meant for work; work is meant for the pioneer."

Chant: Zum ga - li ga - li ga - li, Zum ga - li ga - li,

Zum ga - li ga - li ga - li, Zum ga - li ga - li,

Solo: He - cha - lutz le - ma - an a - vo - dah; ___

Chant: Zum ga - li ga - li, Zum ga - li ga - li,

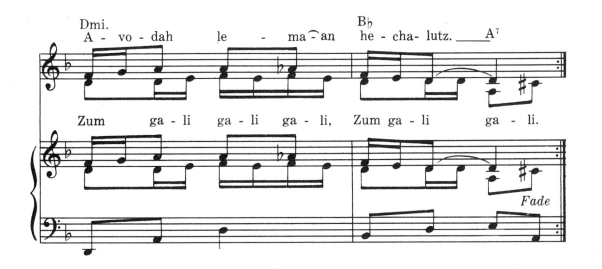

A - vo-dah le - ma͡an he - cha-lutz. ___

Zum ga-li ga-li ga-li, Zum ga-li ga-li.

Fade

Ducks on a Pond

Moderately

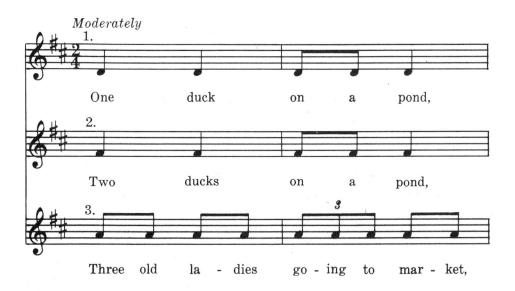

1. One duck on a pond,

2. Two ducks on a pond,

3. Three old la - dies go - ing to mar - ket,

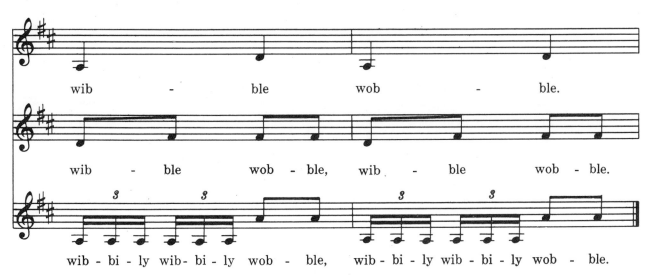

wib - ble wob - ble.

wib - ble wob - ble, wib - ble wob - ble.

wib - bi - ly wib - bi - ly wob - ble, wib - bi - ly wib - bi - ly wob - ble.

Sweet Potatoes

A Creole folk song with a simple and beautiful descant—a perfect song for group harmonizing.

Smoothly

DESCANT:
Roo, roo, roo, roo, Hoo roo, Sing

TUNE:
1. Soon as we all cook sweet po - ta - toes, sweet po - ta - toes,
2. Soon as sup - per's et, Mam - my hol - lers, Mam - my hol - lers,

ho - de - dink - um! Roo, roo, roo, roo, Hoo
sweet po - ta - toes, Soon as we all cook sweet po - ta - toes,
Mam - my hol - lers, Soon as sup - per's et, Mam - my hol - lers,

roo,   hoo   roo! _____

eat 'em right straight up. _____
"Get a - long   to   bed!" _____

3. Soon's we touch our heads to the pillow,
   To the pillow, to the pillow,
   Soon's we touch our heads to the pillow,
   Go to sleep right smart.

Descant: *(to go with all verses)*
       Roo, roo roo roo,
       Hoo roo,
       Sing ho-de-dink-um!
       Roo, roo roo roo,
       Hoo roo, hoo roo!

4. Soon's the rooster crow in the morning,
   In the morning, in the morning,
   Soon's the rooster crow in the morning,
   Gotta wash our face.

Sarasponda

A twopart song of nonsense syllables.

Rollicking
G

DESCANT:

Bun - da bun - da bun - da bun - da bun - da bun - da bun - da bun - da

TUNE:

Sa - ra - spon - da, sa - ra - spon - da, sa - ra - spon - da, rut - sut - sut.

Bun - da bun - da bun - da bun - da bun - da bun - da bun - da bun - da

Sa - ra - spon - da, sa - ra - spon - da, sa - ra - spon - da, rut - sut - sut. A-

One Bottle of Pop

With a swinging rhythm

1. One bot-tle of pop, Two bot-tle of pop, Three bot-tle of pop,

2. Don't throw your junk in my back - yard, My back - yard,

3. Fish and chips and vin - e - gar, Vin - e - gar,

Four bot-tle of pop, Five bot-tle of pop, Six bot-tle of pop,

my back - yard. Don't throw your junk in my back - yard.

vin - e - gar, Fish and chips and vin - e - gar,

Sev - en bot-tle of pop, Pop!

My back - yard's full.

Vin - e - gar, Pop!

PART X
HELLO, GOODBYE, HURRAY FOR US!

Songs for arriving, cheering, waiting, and leaving

The Campbells Are Coming

An old song from the eighteenth-century Scottish rebellion adapted for use as a greeting song, especially to mark the arrival of a latecomer to the group. Any name may be used instead of "the Campbells": "the counselors," "the Robinsons," "Mr. Seeger," etc.

So let's give a hear-ty good cheer. (Hoo-ray!) Now loud-er, or they might not

hear. (Hoo-ray!) The Camp-bells are com-ing, And that's why we're sing-ing. The

Camp-bells are com-ing, o ho, o ho.

We're All Gonna Shine Tonight

The name of a school, camp, group, or person may be substituted for "we're all" in this familiar rallying song.

Spiritedly

We're all ___ gon-na shine to-night, we're all ___ gon-na shine.

We're all ___ gon-na shine to-night, all down ___ the line.

We're all ___ dressed up to-night; we're feel - ing fine. When the
sun goes down and the moon comes up, We're all gon - na shine.

Vive l'Amour

"Hurrah for love and hurrah for all of us," says the refrain of this well-known old drinking song. "Vive" is here pronounced "vee-vuh"; "l'amour" is pronounced "la-moor"; "compagnie" is pronounced "com-pahn-yee."

Vivace   F

1. Let ev - 'ry good fel - low now join in a song.
2. A friend on the left and a friend on the right;

C⁷   F

Vi - ve la com - pa - gnie! _____ Suc - cess to each oth - er, and
In love and good - fel - low - ship

pass it a - long.
let us u - nite.

C⁷   F

Vi - ve la com - pa - gnie!

Vi - ve l'a -, vi - ve l'a, vi - ve l'a - mour; Vi - ve l'a -, vi - ve l'a,

vi - ve l'a - mour; Vi - ve l'a - mour, vi - ve l'a - mour,

Vi - ve la com - pa - gnie! ____

We Won't Go Home Until Morning

Here is an old favorite with a new tune.

Adamantly

We won't go home un - til mor - ning, _____ We won't go home un - til mor - ning, _____ We won't go home un - til mor - ning, _____ Till

day - light does ___ ap - pear. ___ Till day - light does ___ ap -

pear, ___ Till day - light does ___ ap - pear; ___ We won't go home un - til

mor - ning, ___ Till day - light does ___ ap - pear. ___

Good Night, Ladies

A traditional song to end festivities with.

Steadily

1. Good night, la - dies; good night, la - dies; Good night, la - dies; we're
2. Sweet dreams, la - dies; sweet dreams, la - dies; Sweet dreams, la - dies; we're

going to leave you now.   *A little faster*   Mer - ri - ly we roll a - long,
going to leave you now.   Mer - ri - ly we roll the keg,

3. Goodbye, ladies; goodbye ladies;
   Goodbye, ladies, we're going to leave you now.
   Merrily we drink it down, drink it down, drink it down;
   Merrily we drink it down until there is no more.

roll a - long, roll a - long; Mer - ri - ly we roll a - long ___
roll the keg, roll the keg; Mer - ri - ly we roll the keg a -

o - ver the deep blue sea.
cross ___ the bar - room floor.

4. Farewell, ladies; farewell, ladies;
   Farewell, ladies; we're going to leave you now.
   Gloomily we roll it back, roll it back, roll it back;
   Gloomily we roll it back, because there ain't no more.

Goodbye, My Lover, Goodbye

*A combination of a sea shanty and a lullaby that has become
a college-campus favorite*

Bouncing

1. The ship is sai - ling down the bay; Good-bye, my lov - er, good- bye;___ We
2. My heart will ev - er - more be true, Good-bye, my lov - er, good- bye;___ Though

may not meet for man - y a day, Good-bye, my lov - er, good- bye.
now we sad - ly say___ a - dieu, Good-bye, my lov - er, good- bye.

Chorus:

Sing - ing a - bye - low, my ba - by,

Bye - low, my boun - cing ba - by boy; Sing - ing a-

bye - low, my ba - by, _____ Good-

bye, my lov - er, good - bye, good - bye, Good - bye, my lov - er good - bye.

3. Though far I roam across the sea,
Goodbye, my lover, goodbye,
My thoughts will ever be with thee,
Goodbye, my lover, goodbye.

Chorus: Singing a-bye-low, my baby,
Bye-low, my bouncing baby boy;
Singing a-bye-low, my baby,
Goodbye, my lover, goodbye, goodbye,
Goodbye, my lover, goodbye.

Auld Lang Syne

We're Here Because We're Here

This old Scottish folk song with words by Robert Burns has become a traditional song of parting among good friends everywhere. "We're Here Because We're Here," sung to the same tune, is the song to begin singing . . . and singing . . . and singing . . . as the train or bus or car nears its destination.

With feeling

1. Should auld ac-quain-tance be for-got And nev-er brought to mind? Should

auld ac-quain-tance be for-got, And days of auld lang syne?

2. And here's a hand, my trusty friend,
   And give a hand of thine;
   We'll take a cup of kindness yet
   For auld lang syne.

Chorus: For auld lang syne, my dear,
   For auld lang syne,
   We'll take a cup of kindness yet
   For auld lang syne.

Chorus:

For auld ___ lang ___ syne, my dear, For auld ___ lang ___ syne, We'll take a cup of kind-ness yet For ___ auld ___ lang ___ syne.

We're Here Because We're Here

We're here because we're here because
We're here because we're here;
We're here because we're here because
We're here because we're here.

Chorus: We're here because we're here because
We're here because we're here;
We're here because we're here because
We're here because we're here.

Bang Bang Bang

An American sea shanty adapted as a group mealtime waiting song. The name of a member of the group may be sung in place of "Johnny"—or, for a camp or school group, the name or number of a table ("Oh table, table one, come along . . ."). The person or group named must stand up and keep a straight face while the song is sung. The other singers, needless to say, do their utmost to make the person or group named laugh, by making faces, etc. At the words "Bang, bang, bang," everybody makes a rhythmic noise with silverware on glasses or cups.

With vigor

Oh, John - ny, John - ny, John, come a - long, come a - long; Oh,

John - ny, John - ny, John, come a - long. Don't stand there like a

sil - ly old   fool;   Don't stand there a - look - ing nice and cool;

Don't be glum and gloom - y.   Let your teeth go Bang! Bang! Bang!

Old Horse

An American sea shanty traditionally sung when the first barrel or "salt horse" (salted beef or pork) was opened on the outward passage, adapted here as a dinnertime waiting song.

Old horse, old horse, we'd have you know That to the kit-chen you must go. The

cook, with-out a sign of grief, Will boil you down and call you beef; And

we poor kids a-stand-ing here Must eat you, though you look so queer. Old

horse, old horse, what brought you here?

Only One More Day

A well-known sea shanty adapted for group singing. This song may be used as a "countdown," with the number changing as the end of school or camp approaches: "Only ten more days of camp, Ten more days . . ." or, for fun, "Only one hundred seventy-six more days of school . . ." Other verses may catalog favorite activities that will come to an end.

On-ly one more day of sum-mer, One more __ day; Oh,

rock and roll me o - ver, One more __ day.

Improvised verses:

Only one more day of swimming,
One more day;
Oh, rock and roll me over,
One more day.
Only one more day of arts and crafts, *etc.*
Only one more day of geometry
(*history, etc., for schools*)

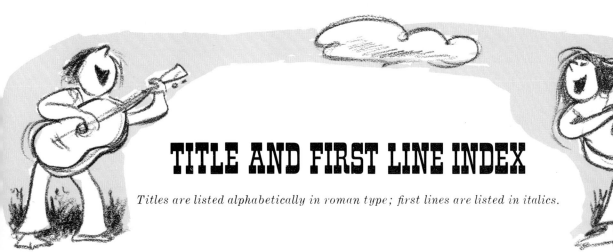

TITLE AND FIRST LINE INDEX

Titles are listed alphabetically in roman type; first lines are listed in italics.